# STAR GAZING

## MOVIES AND ASTROLOGY

# ELEANOR RINGEL

LONGSTREET
Atlanta, Georgia

Published by
LONGSTREET PRESS, INC.
A subsidiary of Cox Newspapers,
A subsidiary of Cox Enterprises, Inc.
2140 Newmarket Parkway
Suite 122
Marietta, GA   30067

Printed in the United States of America

Library of Congress Catalog Card Number:  98-066366

ISBN 1-56352-493-7

Jacket and book design by Burtch Hunter
Typesetting by Jill Dible

*To my shining star, my husband John.*

## Acknowledgments

To Kathy Trocheck, who said just do it; Terry Kay, who said here's how; Chuck Perry, who said yes; and Emma Edmonds and Tad Williams, who listened.

# STAR GAZING

## MOVIES AND ASTROLOGY

To Katharine
A happy-go-lucky &
ever-lucky Sag. Keep
having those Adventures
Best,
Eloise

# INTRODUCTION

*"The fault, dear Brutus, is not in our stars,*
*but in ourselves, that we are underlings."*
 — Julius Caesar, Act 1, Scene 11.

Stargazing was part of human nature long before the first movie camera ever rolled. Before we worshipped such heavenly creatures as Charlie Chaplin and Marilyn Monroe, Leonardo DiCaprio and Julia Roberts, we looked to the skies for Virgo and Aquarius, Leo and Pisces.

I am not an astrologer, and I don't play one on TV. Or in the newspaper. But after twenty years of writing about the movies — and devoutly checking my daily horoscope — I began to wonder if there might indeed be some connection between the heavenly stars and the Hollywood stars. Now, those who cast horoscopes for a living will tell you there's a lot more to it than simply assigning a sun sign. But it's certainly a good start, and some of the matches I found were downright startling.

Aries, the warrior-Ram, just so happens to be the sign of Ewan McGregor, George Lucas' designated Star Warrior for the Twenty-first Century.

Capricorn comic Jim Carrey has the same birthday (January 17) as Capricorn comic Andy Kaufman, whom he's playing in his next film, "Man on the Moon."

And consider how many nimble artists were born under the athletically inclined sign of Sagittarius: swashbuckling Douglas Fairbanks Jr., martial-arts master Bruce Lee and extravagant choreographer Busby Berkeley.

Originally, this book was meant to be more of a consumer guide. Sort of, if I'm a Gemini, should I rent "The Remains of the Day?" (well, you could, but it's better suited to service-oriented Virgos; you Geminis might be happier with the bouncing-off-the-wall antics of "Who Framed Roger Rabbit?" or the twin weirdness of "Dead Ringers.").

There are still plenty of suggestions along those lines. But the more research I did, the more evidence I found that stars can be as star-crossed as they are star-blessed. Richard Burton's flamboyant addictions can't help but suggest his Scorpio birthright, while Jim Henson's optimistic, follow-the-rainbow alter ego, Kermit the Frog, is a pure Libra (as was Henson).

Finally, even if you don't buy into horoscopes whole-heartedly, it seems like it's got to be more than mere coincidence that MGM's famous symbol, Leo the Lion, first roared on screen under the sign of — what else? — Leo.

*Who works from morn to set of Sun*
 *And never likes to be outdone?*
 *Whose walk is almost like a run?*
  *Who? Aries.*
*Who smiles through life except when crossed?*
 *Who knows or thinks he knows the most?*
 *Who loves good things: baked, boiled or roast?*
  *Oh, Taurus.*
*Who's fond of life and jest and pleasure:*
 *Who vacillates and changes ever?*
 *Who loves attention without measure?*
  *Why, Gemini.*
*Who changes like a changeful season:*
 *Holds fast and lets go without reason?*
 *Who is there to give adhesion*
  *To Cancer?*
*Who praises all his kindred do:*

*Expects his friends to praise them too —*
*And cannot see their senseless view?*
*Ah, Leo.*
*Who criticizes all she sees:*
*Yes, e'en would analyze a sneeze?*
*Who hugs and loves her own disease?*
*Humph, Virgo.*
*Who puts you off with promise gay,*
*And keeps you waiting half the day?*
*Who compromises all the way?*
*Sweet Libra.*
*Who keeps an arrow in his bow,*
*And if you prod, he lets it go?*
*A fervent friend, a subtle foe —*
*Scorpio.*
*Who loves the dim religious light:*
*Who always keeps a star in sight?*
*An Optimist both gay and bright-*
*Sagittarius.*
*Who climbs and schemes for wealth and place,*
*And mourns his brother's fall from grace —*
*But takes what's due in any case —*
*Safe Capricorn.*
*Who gives to all a helping hand,*
*But bows his head to no command —*
*And higher laws doth understand?*
*Inventor, Genius, Superman —*
*Aquarius.*
*Who prays and serves and prays some more;*
*And feeds the beggar at the door —*
*And weeps o'er love lost long before?*
*Poor Pisces.*

— Joseph Addison (1672–1719)

# STAR GAZING

## MOVIES AND ASTROLOGY

# ARIES

## MARCH 21 — APRIL 19

The number of high-profile movie people born under Aries is staggering. Try Marlon Brando, Alec Baldwin, Doris Day and Eddie Murphy — all born on April 3. Not convinced? How about Spencer Tracy, Bette Davis, Gregory Peck, Melvyn Douglas and Roger Corman? Same story. Same day (April 5). But then, those with the Ram as their sun sign are born with the raw material that often makes movie stars. They're fiery, headstrong whirlwinds, unafraid of taking a risk or meeting a challenge. They're also extremely competitive with a "me-first" attitude that certainly doesn't hurt when fighting for roles in an overcrowded profession.

Even their weaknesses work in Hollywood — like their predilection for butting heads or a tendency to start a project without bothering to see it through (ever wonder why so many projects go into turn-around or are terminated because of "creative differences"?)

Rams are hard-headed, so they don't give up easily. They're also born leaders, which makes them as at ease calling the shots from behind the camera as they are dominating the spotlight. Aries directors include David Lean, Quentin Tarantino, Curtis Hanson, Charles Burnett, Andre Tarkovsky, Stanley Donen, Alan J. Pakula, Barry Levinson and Francis Ford Coppola.

Energetic, pioneering, ambitious and pretty much unstoppable; that's Aries. Does it surprise you that Charlie Chaplin is one? So is Ewan MacGregor.

The Aries movie-lover is likewise fearless in his or her choices. There are few films they won't at least give a look, but they're naturally drawn to adventures, war movies, or even something like the oh-so-'90s "William Shakespeare's Romeo and Juliet," starring Aries beauty Claire Danes and someone named Leo. What to avoid? Nothing really, but a gooey love story (like, say, "Love Story") may not be a first choice. And let someone else worry with the social-issue flicks. Aries are out to conquer the world, not save it.

## FIVE SUGGESTED RENTALS

**"Apollo 13"** (1996)
Tom Hanks and director Ron Howard shoot the moon in this unexpectedly gripping and entertaining retelling of the moon landing that wasn't. In 1970, less than a year after Neil Armstrong made his one small step for man, Apollo 13 is lunar-bound under the command of Jim Lovell (Hanks). His crew includes Fred Haise (Bill Paxton) and Jack Swigert (Kevin Bacon). All goes well until the third day, when Lovell tells Houston, "We've got a problem." How do Howard and his cast make us forget we're watching a foregone conclusion? Simple. By making this an actor's movie. Despite all the techno-jargon and the painstakingly re-created lunar module, the picture comes down to one thing: Do these guys have the right stuff?

They do, and how they show us they do is the stuff Aries' fantasies are made of. As Lovell tells his colleagues, "Gentlemen, it's been a privilege flying with you."

**"Glengarry Glen Ross"** (1992)
Stress is made flesh in David Mamet's scathingly brilliant dark comedy about a cut-throat gang of real estate salesmen who'd sell the Brooklyn Bridge to their own mothers. Based on Mamet's prize-winning play, the movie is a mesmerizing actors' showcase, with characters as repellant as they are fascinating. Among those spewing Mamet's rat-a-tat expletive-laden dialogue are Al Pacino as a crafty, confident shark with a line for every sucker; Jack Lemmon as Pacino's former mentor, now a worn-out Willy Loman; Kevin Spacey as the wily, officious office manager; and Alec Baldwin as the guy sent by the front office to accelerate the stress-factor (top salesman gets a car; second gets steak knives; everyone else gets the boot). This is a battleground familiar to every Aries and the fascination is less in who wins or loses but in how the game is played. Ruthlessly.

**"Glory"** (1989)
This superb Civil War film relates the little-known story of the fighting 54th, the first all-black military unit in the U.S. Army. Director Edward Zwick takes us from the group's formation to its courageous assault on an impregnable Southern fort. Though the on-going tragedy of racism is a major theme, this is first and foremost a soldier's movie, reminscent of John Ford's cavalry classics. Aries will be drawn to the film's fighting spirit and to its celebration of grace under all sorts of fire, from the obstacles faced by the regiment's white commander (Matthew Broderick) to the very different set of problems confronting the company's disparate black volunteers, led by Denzel Washington and Morgan Freeman. The picture probably deserves a red badge of courage just for getting made in Hollywood, but

it actually won three Oscars, including a Best Supporting Actor award for Washington.

### "The River Wild" (1994)

In this rip-roaring action film/family drama, Meryl Streep, David Straithairn and Kevin Bacon prove it *is* possible to brandish a gun and still pull off some pretty impressive acting. Streep, a former white-water guide and her workaholic husband (Straithairn) take their troubled marriage into rocky waters when they arrange a rafting vacation with their son. Shooting rapids is hard enough; far more dangerous is a suspiciously charming river rat (Bacon). Director Curtis Hanson, who came into his own a few years later with the Oscar-winnning "L.A. Confidential," confidently handles this genre mix of family drama and thrill-a-minute action stuff. Streep takes to the Aries leader/hero role as if she were learning a new accent. Looking fit enough to handle the bad guys in "Deliverance," she could make Ahnuld and Clint feel like they're up a creek without a paddle.

### "The Bridge on the River Kwai" (1957)

If you haven't seen it, you should. If you have seen it, see it again. A trio of gifted Aries — director David Lean and stars William Holden and Sir Alec Guiness — help make this one of the films that always comes up when film buffs are listing classics. It's the story of soldiers caught on a very different battlefront. Guiness is a stiff-upper-lipped British colonel who heads a contingent of American and British prisoners of war being held in a steaming jungle camp during World War II. The camp's Japanese commander, Sessue Hayakawa, orders the construction of a bridge, setting the stage for a gripping drama/character study — Guiness and Hayakawa clash repeatedly — as well as a heck of an action film as Holden escapes the camp and returns with orders to blow up the bridge. It is a very-Aries look at issues of leadership and Guiness's misguidedness is magnificent.

## SIX TALENTED ARIES

### Marlon Brando (April 3, 1924)

There is only one Marlon Brando, and both his admirers and his critics would likely agree that one is enough. With typical Aries self-assurance, he charged onto the screen in the early '50s and forever changed the face of movie acting. Since his early successes, such as "A Streetcar Named Desire," "On the Waterfront" and "The Wild One," his career has had its ups and downs, its embarrassing clunkers ("Mutiny on the Bounty") and its astonishing come-backs ("The Godfather"). Yet in his bloated twilight, he remains one of our movie gods — a brute-angel in a torn t-shirt or a regretfully murderous Mafia don in elegant tux and black tie. Even in his self-imposed South Seas exile, he remains a phenomenon — volatile, charismatic, ultimately unknowable. An inteviewer asked him early in his career if he was mad, and Brando responded sweetly, "Only when the moon is full."

**Suggested Rental:** "The Godfather" (1972)

It is, quite simply, one of the greatest movies ever made. Working from Mario Puzo's best-seller, director Francis Ford Coppola (another Aries) portrays the Mafia as a business. More important, however, he portrays it as a family at a time when the nuclear family seemed to be falling to pieces after the upheavals of the '60s. The rest of the country may be going to hell in a hippie handbasket, but you could still count on the Mob to get things done. Brando is the courtly, yet ruthless, patriarch committed to building an illegal empire that he hopes to pass on to one of his sons (James Caan, Al Pacino, John Cazale). While Brando's presence permeates the film, the actual Aries figure is Caan's (also an Aries) impulsive, hot-headed Sonny. And we all know how he ends up.

**Aries Moment:** When Coppola was casting the film, Brando

was pretty much a Hollywood pariah. Brando made a screen test, which he he hadn't done in more than a decade. He stained his hair white, slicked it back, used shoe polish to create dark circles under his eyes and, most famously, stuffed his cheeks with tissue paper. The suits who saw the test loved it, and they didn't even recognize him. Talk about Aries enterprise.

## Warren Beatty (March 30, 1937)

Michelle Phillips, one of Warren Beatty's numerous former flames, perhaps put it best when she told an interviewer, "When Warren Beatty wants you to like him, there's no way not to like him." Aries men are among the most virile and seductive males on the planet — all that conquest stuff concentrated into the battle of the sexes. Beatty has made some of the most respected films of all time in his lengthy career, including "Bonnie and Clyde," "McCabe and Mrs. Miller," "Shampoo," "Heaven Can Wait," "Reds" and "Dick Tracy." Yet what people tend to think about first when his name comes up are all those other names: Julie (Christie), Leslie (Caron), Natalie (Wood), Diane (Keaton) and Madonna, to name a few. Marriage to Annette Bening and parenthood may have settled him down off screen, but on screen he remains the same — the impossibly handsome, impossibly charming movie star.

**Suggested Rental:** "Bonnie and Clyde" (1967)
Forget "Easy Rider." Here are the true desperado icons of the '60s. Though set in the depression '30s, when the real Bonnie Parker (Faye Dunaway) and Clyde Barrow (Warren Beatty) robbed banks on their crime spree across the country's midsection, this groundbreaking classic is redolent with the humor, violence and sheer craziness of the late '60s. Cowritten by Robert Benton (who later became an Oscar-

winning director), shrewdly directed by Arthur Penn and produced by Beatty, the movie puts what was then called the generation gap on screen. The youth of America identified more with the glamorous outlaws than with their victims or the various authority figures trying to trap them. Critics — most of them on the older side of said gap — roundly condemned it. But Bonnie and Clyde were a new kind of leader for a new kind of battle.

**Aries Moment:** Beatty first considered Bonnie and Clyde's story with himself and then-girlfriend, Leslie Caron, in mind. Then he decided she wasn't right for the role. Caron later said, "The way he discarded me . . . was rather ruthless." Well, Aries, you do have that "me-first" streak. Ironically, Caron was instrumental in getting Beatty to buy the script in the first place.

### Emma Thompson (April 15, 1959)

Early in her career, Emma Thompson existed in her famous husband's shadow, despite her own talents. It was always, Kenneth Branagh and . . . She soon came into her own, though, not only performing in her now ex-husband's films — "Henry V," "Much Ado About Nothing" and "Peter's Friends" — but also in movies that had nothing to do with him, such as "Howard's End," "The Tall Guy," "Sense and Sensibility" and "In the Name of the Father." As she scooped up parts and awards (an Oscar for "Howard's End"), it became clear she had more to offer than being the other half of a famous acting duo. Her Aries side manifests itself in her willingness to take risks, rather than sticking with the sort of corseted nineteenth-century heroines that made her famous. Her portrayal of a smart, ambitious political wife in "Primary Colors" is less a Hillary impersonation than a superb portrait of Aries leadership lust and killer instinct.

**Suggested Rental:** "Junior" (1994)
The Terminator becomes the Incubator in this light-hearted look at maternity, Ahnuld-style. Schwarzenegger stars as a dedicated scientist who, along with partner, Danny DeVito, invents a drug to aid difficult pregnancies. When the FDA refuses to let them test it, they do what all movie doctors do: test it in secret on themselves. DeVito puts an embryo fertilized with Arnold's manly sperm into his manly abdomen. But when the agreed-upon twelve weeks pass — the time to abort the experiment — the daddy-to-be decides he wants his baby. His body, his choice! Thompson plays another scientist who's more involved with Arnold than she realizes. The movie gets a little dopey when Arnold starts behaving like a sitcom cliche - worrying about what to wear, nagging DeVito, etc. But overall, it's amiable good fun. And talk about a pioneering Aries spirit . . . he truly does go where no man has gone before.

**Aries Moment:** Thompson's supporting role was hardly the sort of challenging stuff people expected from an Oscar winner. But Thompson explained she took the role because the film "seemed to me to have every hope of offending a great number of people. And I don't think there's any point in making a comedy unless there's a possibility of offending a great number of people." That's Aries for you. Give 'em a challenge, and they can't say no.

# Eddie Murphy (April 3, 1961)

They dubbed him "Crazy Eddie" and why not? The trademark brashness is pure Aries. So is the self-confident grin and the emphatically headstrong behavior on and off screen. Eddie Murphy stood out the minute he stood in front of a camera on "Saturday Night Live." A year after his network debut, he was making movies, first playing a fast-talking con man paired with Nick Nolte's stolid cop in "48 Hours." After a string of hits stretching from "Trading Places" to "Coming to America," his career and his reputation nose-dived. There were rumors that he was difficult, arrogant, volatile – the usual downside-of-Aries complaints. But then he turned an old Jerry Lewis vehicle, "The Nutty Professor," into a major comeback. And as for that stuff about being a 4 A.M. Good Samaritan to a transvestite hooker, well, Aries folks are known to act before they think.

**Suggested Rental:** "Beverly Hills Cop" (1984)
This crowd-pleaser firmly established the Eddie Murphy persona. When his best friend is murdered, Detroit detective Axel Foley (Murphy) decides to soak up some rays – and sniff out some leads – in Beverly Hills, where his pal was hanging out before his death. What makes the film so much fun isn't the whodunit part (it's about as suspenseful as guessing who'll be back for the next season of "Saturday Night Live"), but watching the mercurial Murphy nimbly navigate any and all obstacles – from a snooty Rodeo Drive salesman (Bronson Pinchot's unforgettable cameo) to a bunch of well-behaved Beverly Hills officers (led by Judge Reinhold), whose idea of a big collar is a parking ticket on a Mercedes. Murphy sacrifices some of his comic lovableness for a leading-man's harder edge. He's not just a cute cut-up; he's an Aries kind of guy, using his own initiative and refusing to always play by the rules.

**Aries Moment:** "Beverly Hills Cop" wasn't exactly the sure thing it looks like in retrospect. The script had been kicking around Hollywood for years and had gone through more than a dozen versions – including one for Mickey Rourke and another for Sylvester Stallone. True, Murphy was at the right place at the right time, but it took his Aries boldness to decide he could make this hybrid of comedy and violence into a hit.

## Steve McQueen (March 24, 1930)

Steve McQueen was the eternal Peck's Bad Boy of the movies. He was tough; he was hip; he was cool. He combined James Dean's loner appeal and little-boy-lost hurt with an action star's machismo. He had that Aries full-speed-ahead attitude. Which may be why, when one thinks of him, he's almost always in motion: tearing up the countryside on that motorcycle in "The Great Escape," bouncing up and down the hilly streets of San Franciso in "Bullitt," or charging helter-skelter up Boot Hill in a horse-drawn hearse in "The Magnificent Seven." He could play quieter roles, too, such as the poker-faced card player in "The Cincinnatti Kid," the sly billionaire thief in "The Thomas Crowne Affair" and the Faulknerian rascal in "The Reivers." But it was a zest for life that he projected so clearly. He was a born Aries fighter who only lost one battle — with lung cancer at age fifty.

**Suggested Rental:** "The Great Escape" (1963)
Perhaps one of the most sheerly enjoyable action movies ever made. Based on Paul Brickhill's book about a real-life daring escape made from a German POW camp during World War ll by a bunch of courageous Allied prisoners, the movie is a veritable who's who of early '60s male star power. Along with McQueen — whose character is nicknamed the Cooler King for his record-breaking number of failed escape attempts — you'll see Charles Bronson as a claustrophobic tunnel digger; James Coburn as a sardonic Aussie; David McCallum as the devoted aid to the camp's big cheese, Richard Attenborough; and James Garner as a smooth hustler who can steal anything from passports to cameras. Directed by John Sturges with an impudent, boys'-adventure spirit, the picture bristles with energy, enterprise and fearlessness. An almost perfect Aries flick.

**Aries Moment:** McQueen's bid for freedom on a stolen motorcycle is probably the movie's most famous sequence. But in typical Aries go-getter style, the actor, who was an expert bike rider in real life, wasn't content just to play his hero's role. He also donned a helmet and uniform and doubled as one of the German soldiers chasing his character.

## Quentin Tarantino (March 27, 1963)

Not many filmmakers become a household name after only two films, but that's exactly what happened to Quentin Tarantino. With that irresistable Aries initiative, he went from video-store clerk to Oscar nominee in less than five years. Both his debut film, "Reservoir Dogs," and his breakthrough hit, "Pulp Fiction," exude pure Aries aggression in their cinematic style, plots, characters and snap-crackle-pop dialogue. Though he has not fared as well since he became an instant superstar — "Four Rooms," "From Dusk Till Dawn," "Destiny Turns on the Radio" and "Jackie Brown" didn't exactly enhance his reputation or his bank account — he's not down for the count yet. Tarantino is an Aries, so he can dish it out. He can take it, too. Besides, if he can single-handedly revive John Travolta's career, he can certainly take care of his own.

**Suggested rental:** "Reservoir Dogs" (1992)
Tarantino's film is an electrifyingly vicious caper flick, soaked in blood, obscenity and incongruous black humor. The movie mostly takes place before and after a diamond heist gone wrong. Dressed in identical "Men in Black" suits and cloaked in the anonymity of color-coded aliases (Mr. White, Mr. Orange, Mr. Pink, etc.), the rattled crooks repair to a warehouse to figure out who ratted on whom and what to do about it. The high-propane ensemble cast — Tim Roth, Harvey Keitel, Chris Penn and Steve Buscemi,

among others — are worthy of a Mamet play (which this film's profane energy often evokes). A violent exercise in head-butting brutality (Aries alert) and antic, neo-Jacobean mayhem, this is a fiercely riveting picture. And you will never, ever think of "Stuck in the Middle with You" in the same way. Promise.

**Aries Moment:** Connoisseurs of Hong-Kong action films noted a certain unmistakable resemblance between the plot of "Reservoir Dogs" and Ringo Lam's 1989 "City on Fire," starring Chow Yun-Fat. At a press conference at Cannes, Tarantino brazened out the accusations with admirable Aries bravado: "I love 'City on Fire' and I have a poster for it framed in my house. It's a great movie. I steal from every movie . . . if my work has anything, it's that I'm taking this from this and that from that and mixing them together . . . I steal from everything. Great artists STEAL, they don't do homages."

## MOVIES "BORN" UNDER ARIES

TARZAN THE APE MAN
SAY ANYTHING
PRETTY WOMAN
THE TEENAGE MUTANT
  NINJA TURTLES
CRY BABY
DEFENDING YOUR LIFE
BASIC INSTINCT
WHITE MEN CAN'T JUMP
FERNGULLY
THE PAPER

THE HUDSUCKER PROXY
SERIAL MOM
DOLORES CLAIBORNE
ROB ROY
FLIRTING WITH DISASTER
JAMES AND THE GIANT
  PEACH
LIAR LIAR
GROSSE POINT BLANK
THE BIG ONE
THE NEWTON BOYS

# OTHER FAMOUS ARIES

**MARCH 21**
Rosie O'Donnell (1962)
Gary Oldman (1958)
Timothy Dalton (1946)
Marie-Christine Barrault (1944)
Françoise Dorleac (1942)
Kathleen Widdoes (1939)
Al Freeman Jr. (1934)
James Coco (1930)
Peter Brook (1925)
Russ Meyer (1922)
Peter Bull (1912)
W. S. Van Dyke (1889)
Bronco Billy Anderson (1882)

**MARCH 22**
Reese Witherspoon (1976)
Matthew Modine (1959)
Lena Olin (1955)
Fanny Ardant (1949)
Bruno Ganz (1941)
Haing S. Ngor (1940)
M. Emmet Walsh (1935)
William Shatner (1931)
Virginia Grey (1917)
Karl Malden (1914)
Joseph Schildkraut (1895)
Chico Marx (1887)

**MARCH 23**
Richard Grieco (1965)
Amanda Plummer (1957)
Trevor Jones (1949)
Mark Rydell (1934)

Ugo Tognazzi (1922)
Akira Kurosawa (1910)
Joan Crawford (1908)

**MARCH 24**
Lara Flynn Boyle (1970)
Annabella Sciorra (1964)
Kelly Le Brock (1960)
Robert Carradine (1954)
Curtis Hanson (1945)
R. Lee Ermey (1944)
Steve McQueen (1930)
Gene Nelson (1920)
Richard Conte (1914)
Ubi Iwerks (1901)
Roscoe "Fatty" Arbuckle (1887)

**MARCH 25**
Sarah Jessica Parker (1965)
Mary Gross (1953)
Elton John (1947)
Bonnie Bedelia (1946)
Aretha Franklin (1942)
Hoyt Axton (1938)
Simone Signoret (1921)
David Lean (1908)

**MARCH 26**
Jennifer Grey (1960)
Martin Short (1950)
Diana Ross (1944)
James Caan (1939)
Alan Arkin (1934)
Leonard Nimoy (1931)

Strother Martin (1919)
Sterling Hayden (1916)

**MARCH 27**
Quentin Tarantino (1963)
Maria Schneider (1952)
Michael York (1942)
Austin Pendleton (1940)
Gloria Swanson (1899)

**MARCH 28**
Vince Vaughn (1970)
Dianne Wiest (1948)
Mike Newell (1943)
Freddie Bartholomew (1924)
Dirk Bogarde (1921)
Flora Robson (1902)

**MARCH 29**
Elle McPherson (1964)
Michael Winterbottom (1961)
Christopher Lambert (1957)
Bud Cort (1948)
Eric Idle (1943)
Eileen Heckert (1919)
Pearl Bailey (1918)
Arthur O'Connell (1906)
Warner Baxter (1889)

**MARCH 30**
Michael Lehmann (1957)
Paul Reiser (1957)
Warren Beatty (1937)
John Astin (1930)
Turhan Bey (1920)

*Ewan McGregor*

**MARCH 31**
Ewan McGregor (1971)
Paul Mercurio (1963)
Christopher Walken (1943)
Richard Chamberlain (1935)
Shirley Jones (1934)
Richard Kiley (1922)

**APRIL 1**
Annette O'Toole (1952)
Ali McGraw (1938)
Debbie Reynolds (1932)
George Grizzard (1928)
Jane Powell (1926)
Toshiro Mifune (1920)
Wallace Beery (1885)
Lon Chaney (1883)

**APRIL 2**
Dana Carvey (1955)
Lili Fini Zanuck (1954)
Pamela Reed (1949)
Linda Hunt (1945)
Diane Cilento (1934)
Alec Guiness (1914)

**APRIL 3**
Eddie Murphy (1961)
David Hyde Pierce (1959)

# ARIES

Alec Baldwin (1958)
Jonathan Lynn (1943)
Marsha Mason (1942)
Wayne Newton (1942)
Marlon Brando (1924)
Doris Day (1924)
Jan Sterling (1921)
Leslie Howard (1893)
Allan Dwan (1885)

## APRIL 4
Jennifer Chambers Lynch (1968)
Robert Downey Jr. (1965)
Aki Karismaki (1957)
Christine Lahti (1950)
Craig T. Nelson (1946)
Andrei Tarkovsky (1932)
Anthony Perkins (1932)
Elizabeth Wilson (1925)
Eva Marie Saint (1924)
Elmer Bernstein (1922)
Eric Rohmer (1920)

## APRIL 5
Michael Moriarty (1941)
Frank Gorshin (1934)
Nigel Hawthorne (1929)
Roger Corman (1926)
Michael V. Gazzi (1923)
Gregory Peck (1916)
Bette Davis (1908)
Melvyn Douglas (1901)
Spencer Tracy (1900)

## APRIL 6
Marilu Henner (1952)

Barry Levinson (1942)
Billy Dee Williams (1938)
Walter Huston (1884)

## APRIL 7
Russell Crowe (1964)
Jackie Chan (1954)
Francis Ford Coppola (1939)
Alan J. Pakula (1928)
James Garner (1928)

## APRIL 8
Patricia Arquette (1968)
Robin Wright (1966)
Doug Trumbull (1942)
John Gavin (1932)
Dorothy Tutin (1930)
Eric Porter (1928)
Edward Mulhare (1923)
Mary Pickford (1892)

*Dennis Quaid*

## APRIL 9
Cynthia Nixon (1966)
Dennis Quaid (1954)
Brandon De Wilde (1942)
Jean-Paul Belmondo (1933)
Ward Bond (1903)
Paul Robson (1898)

**APRIL 10**
Peter MacNichol (1954)
Steven Seagal (1952)
Omar Sharif (1932)
Max Von Sydow (1929)
Harry Morgan (1915)
Tim McCoy (1891)
George Arliss (1868)

**APRIL 11**
Peter Riegert (1947)
John Milius (1944)
Louise Lasser (1939)
Joel Grey (1932)
Johnny Sheffield (1931)
Carl Franklin (1930)
Paul Douglas (1907)

*Claire Danes*

**APRIL 12**
Claire Danes (1979)
Andy Garcia (1956)
Hardy Kruger (1928)
Jane Withers (1925)
David Letterman (1947)

**APRIL 13**
Rick Schroeder (1970)
Ron Perlman (1950)
Charles Burnett (1944)

Paul Sorvino (1939)
Edward Fox (1937)
Stanley Donen (1924)
Howard Keel (1917)

**APRIL 14**
Sarah Michelle Gellar (1977)
Anthony Michael Hall (1968)
Robert Carlyle (1961)
Julie Christie (1941)
Bradford Dillman (1930)
Rod Steiger (1925)
John Gielgud (1904)

**APRIL 15**
Emma Thompson (1959)
Amy Wright (1950)
Lois Chiles (1947)
Robert Walker Jr. (1940)
Claudia Cardinale (1939)
Michael Ansara (1922)
Hans Conreid (1917)
Wallace Reid (1891)

*Ellen Barkin*

**APRIL 16**
Jon Cryer (1965)
Martin Lawrence (1965)
Ellen Barkin (1954)
Jay O. Sanders (1953)

Paul Cox (1940)
Henry Mancini (1924)
Peter Ustinov (1921)
Charles Chaplin (1889)

## APRIL 17
Lela Rochon (1966)
Sean Bean (1959)
Olivia Hussey (1951)
Lindsay Anderson (1923)
William Holden (1916)

## APRIL 18
Eric Roberts (1956)
Rick Moranis (1953)
James Woods (1947)
Hayley Mills (1946)
Robert Hooks (1937)
Miklos Rozsa (1907)

## APRIL 19
Ashley Judd (1968)
Tim Curry (1946)
Dudley Moore (1935)
Jayne Mansfield (1933)
Hugh O'Brian (1925)
Constance Talmadge (1900)

# TAURUS

## APRIL 20 — MAY 20

Steadfast, down-to-earth and centered are all words that come to mind when describing those born under the sign of Taurus the Bull. Conversely, so do words like bull-headed, stubborn and inflexible.

However, the key word for Taurus is "focus." Taureans have their eyes on the prize — whether it's an Oscar or a home in Malibu — and once fixed, they rarely waver. A career in movies might initially seem too quixotic for such a practical, risk-avoiding type. But the built-in difficulties of such a path appeal to Taurus. So do the trappings of stardom — luxury, recognition and the good life.

Taureans are builders by nature. That's why so many of them have managed to achieve lengthy careers in a business that's the equivalent of a sand trap. Quite simply, they aren't quitters and their tenacious nature makes them able to remain undistracted by all the craziness that surrounds them. Among the more famous Hollywood stars born under the Bull are Fred

Astaire, Henry Fonda, Gary Cooper, Jack Nicholson, Jessica Lange, Barbra Streisand, Carol Burnett, Candice Bergen, Bing Crosby and both Hepburns (Audrey and Katharine).

George Lucas built "Star Wars" from a personal fantasy into a world-wide phenomenon. Cher and Dennis Hopper built their unlikely careers by creating and discarding identities to suit the decade. Orson Welles became a Hollywood outcast after his early successes, so he built a career out of *being* an outcast.

The Taurus movie-lover, while having a good sense of humor, just isn't all that interested in frivolous films. Begging Taurean Ann-Margret's pardon, but "Viva Las Vegas" isn't really Taurus's thing. More to their tastes are pictures that celebrate a certain tenacity, whether they're heroic like "High Noon" or "A Man for All Seasons" (both directed by Taurean Fred Zinnemann) or antiheroic like "North Dallas Forty" or "The Godfather, Part II." And don't forget that luxury-loving side. Think Audrey Hepburn and "Breakfast at Tiffany's." Get the picture?

## FIVE SUGGESTED RENTALS

**"Babe"** (1995)
We've seen Porky and Miss Piggy and the Three Little Pigs, but the biggest porker to hit the movies in recent memory is Babe, the little piggie that could. And who just wouldn't quit. A totally Taurean tale of polite persistence, the movie is about a piglet named Babe (voice by Christine Cavanaugh) who's brought home by Farmer Hoggett (James Cromwell) to be fattened up for Christmas dinner. Instead, he's "adopted" by a Border Collie (voice by Miriam Margolyes) and soon he wants to do what his foster family does — herd sheep. The real-life animals carry the bulk of the story, but they get considerable high-tech help from eleborate computer graphics and animatronic stand-ins. Deliciously eccentric and totally

charming, this unique film's success mirrored that of its porcine protagonist; it became the little picture that could, scoring hugely with audiences and critics alike and earning six Oscar nominations.

### "City of Industry" (1997)

Largely ignored in theaters, this neonoir thriller certainly deserves a second chance on video. Harvey Keitel plays a seasoned crook who, after a robbery, goes looking for his former partner (Stephen Dorff, an incendiary mix of ego, amorality and just plain nastiness). And given the mood Keitel is in, Dorff understandably doesn't want to be found. Keitel is playing yet another variation of the screen persona he honed in movies like "Pulp Fiction" and "The Bad Lieutenant" – the seasoned pro with the flip-out edge. The movie has the feel of a perverse quest as the chase takes the lead characters through L.A.'s underbelly. Ultimately, wrongs are righted, rights are restored, and a sunset, however polluted, awaits to be ridden off into. Taureans may not love Keitel altogether, but they"ll admire his seen-it-all self-control and death-before-defeat tenacity.

### "Silkwood" (1983)

Most people probably don't remember nuclear martyr Karen Silkwood who was killed in a mysterious car wreck in 1974 while on her way to talk to a journalist about safety violations at the nuclear processing plant where she worked. However, this movie isn't about her death but movingly and triumphantly about her life. Director Mike Nichols and star Meryl Streep created a character study of a working-class heroine rather than an antinuke propoganda piece. Not born a hero – the Karen we first meet would rather have her breasts raised than her consciousness – she achieves heroism through her self-transformation. The excellent supporting cast includes Kurt Russell and Cher (in her first "acting" role, she earned an Oscar nomination). Taureans will find Karen's blue-collar materialism amusing and will admire her ultimately tragic bull-headedness.

### "Hamburger Hill" (1987)

This can aptly be described as the sort of punch-in-the-face B-movie the late Sam Fuller might've made about Vietnam, if he'd ever gotten around to it. Instead, director John Irvin plunks us down in the middle of combat hell and rubs our face in the mud and blood. On May 10, 1969, the 101st Airborne was sent to take a heavily fortified hill. Ten days and mounds of dead bodies later, they did. The film is about these soldier boys (truly boys; the average age was 19) — the ones who tried, the ones who died, the ones who survived. This is you-are-there filmmaking, with no frills and no "greater" themes. In fact, the entire second hour is nothing but the battle. Taureans will be drawn to its stubborn plainness, its deliberatness and its respect for traditional military heroism, no matter what the consequences. Honest and straightforward, this movie spills its guts for a good cause.

### "Babette's Feast" (1987)

As the world-class gastronomes of the zodiac, Taureans will adore this delectable celebration of the transforming power of art rendered in mouth-wateringly edible terms. Gabriel Axel's Oscar-winning adaptation of an Isak Dinesen novella concerns a French woman (Stephane Audran) who flees the 1871 upheavals in Paris and finds refuge in a remote Danish village where she quietly labors for fourteen years for two pious sisters. Then she wins the lottery and spends all her money on preparations for "a real French dinner" for the sisters and the aging flock they inherited from their late minister father. As the ascetic Danes become the satiated victims of French sensuality, we see how the communal joy of sharing good food can be as soul replenishing as doing good works. Told with an elegant dry wit and just a pinch of regret, this is a four-star feast, a film to savor from soup to nuts.

## SIX TALENTED TAUREANS

### Barbra Streisand (April 24, 1942)

Barbra Streisand is so totally Taurean it's almost scary. On one hand, she's a scrappy, tenacious kid from Brooklyn who wouldn't take no for an answer and wouldn't let anyone else tell her what to do. She wasn't conventionally pretty. So what? She should have a nose job. No way. She kept at it and became an award-winning movie star and one of the most powerful women in Hollywood. The flip side to her Taurus self is her "like buttah" love of luxury. From the fabulous nails to the fabulously furnished homes, she fully indulges her Taurean sensuality and materialism. She's been dirt poor and she's been filthy rich and she knows rich is better. As for that famous perfectionism, that's just another word for Taurus's bull-headedness. She knows what she wants, and she thinks she knows how to get it better than anyone else around. The thing is, she's usually right.

**Suggested Rental:** "Yentl" (1983)

The erstwhile Funny Girl proves she'd make a fine boy and, more important, a very fine director. Streisand makes an unexpectedly self-assured directorial debut with this large-scale musical fable based on the Isaac Bashevis Singer story about a bright, Jewish girl in turn-of-the-century Eastern Europe who disguises herself as a boy so she can study at a yeshiva (a Hebrew school). With its twin motifs of sexual disguise and Jewish life this could've been "Tootsie on the Roof," but the director/star's delight in and commitment to the material is as fervent and appealing as Yentl's thirst for knowledge (it's also very Taurus). Mandy Patinkin is robust and warm as the rabbinical student for whom the disguised Yentl falls, and Amy Irving is almost perfect as the model Jewish daughter who opens Yentl's eyes to a more positive side of the traditional female role.

**Taurus Moment:** As powerful as she was, Streisand was turned down by every studio in town when she approached them with this project. She shopped it for almost a decade before finally getting financial backing. Her one-time lover Jon Peters recalls that they were working together on "The Main Event" when he told her to forget "Yentl. "He insisted, "You're not going to ruin your life and mine. You can't play a boy. We're gonna do something else together. . . ." According to Peters, Streisand sized him up and replied, "Just because you said that, I'm going to do the movie, no matter what." Oy, you Taurus!

### Daniel Day-Lewis (April 29, 1957)

Talented and intense, Daniel Day-Lewis can give Robert De Niro a run for his money when it comes to shape-shifting for a role. He was hunky and long-haired in "The Last of the Mohicans" and effetely repressed and very, very proper in "The Age of Innocence." In "My Left Foot," he twisted himself into the contorted body of poet and cerebral-palsy sufferer Christy Brown. He's been a gay Cockney thug ("My Beautiful Laundrette") and a dandy in pince-nez glasses ("Room with a View"). He was straightforward and heroic in "The Crucible" and a ne'er-do-well troublemaker in "In the Name of the Father." With his Taurus love of building things, he seems to approach each new role as if it were a construction site — something to be worked at from the ground up. To call his performances transformations doesn't really do them justice; they're veritable edifices.

**Suggested Rental:** "My Left Foot" (1989)
Day-Lewis won a much-deserved Oscar for his stunning portrayal of Christy Brown, the Dublin writer and painter so severely crippled by cerebral palsy that the only part of his

twisted body he could control was his left foot. But forget those standard studio-made "saintly disabled" flicks. Christy is a handful first, handicapped second — a brilliant, contentious, flirtacious Irishman with a taste for the bottle and, believe it or not, the occasional brawl. The movie is sentimental (about the Irish, not the disabled), but there's a flinty directness as well (a typical Taurus combination). The star gives a triumph-of-the-will performance, shaking off our pity with a fierce glare and a spittle-ridden oath. Like Christy, the movie is witty, wily and absolutely full of itself. It's as bracing as a good slug of Irish whiskey and every bit as satisfying.

**Taurus Moment:** As he does for all his films, Day-Lewis remained insistently in character every day of the shoot, whether he was on camera or not. Since, as Christy, he could only use his left foot, he had to be fed by the crew on lunch breaks and, if there was no wheelchair around, carried by them over cables and other assorted on-set obstacles. The totality of his commitment wasn't universally beloved (especially at dinner when he stayed in character at restaurants . . . yuuuck) but he never wavered, and his tenaciousness is central to his portrayal.

## Jessica Lange (April 20, 1949)

Think of the determination it takes to transform yourself from the girl in the big hairy paw (i.e., the blonde-bimbo heroine of the disastrous 1976 remake of "King Kong") into a two-time Oscar winner. Jessica Lange is a true Taurus success story — a down-to-earth beauty who refused to be typecast by her porcelain skin and flawless features. After "Kong," which was supposed to be her big break, she didn't work for two years. Some break. Someone less grounded (less Taurus) would've packed it in, but she rebuilt her career one role at a time: the enigmatic angel of death in "All That Jazz;" the sizzling adultress in "The Postman Always Rings Twice;" the self-defeating neurotic actress in "Frances;" and a creamy Patsy Cline in "Sweet Dreams." She won her first Oscar as a soap actress in "Tootsie" and her second as a sensual loose cannon in "Blue Sky." There could be a third in her future.

**Suggested Rental:** "Country" (1984)
Man-killing torandoes and land-eating government agencies are enough to make life a real hoe-downer for Jewel and Gil Ivy (Lange and her longtime lover, Sam Shepard). Faced with foreclosure, Gil starts tending the bar instead of tending to the livestock. But Jewel digs in her heels and fights back. (perhaps she, too, is a Taurus). Like a Midwest Mother Courage (or a cornbelt Norma Rae), she rallies her family and neighbors against the bureaucrats. The movie is rather like the farm people it's about — decent, hard-working, solid and not offering much in the way of surprises. Yet it also has spirit and commitment and some very fine performances. Lange, who snagged another Best Actress nomination with this film, continues to flaunt her range, even at this comparatively early stage of her career. Chances are, if they ever do another remake of "King Kong," she could probably play the title role if she set her mind to it.

**Taurus Moment:** Lange chose this project to launch her second career as a producer. So, not only did she have the burden of the starring role, but she also got a taste of a producer's woes, which included three directors, two studios and the coldest winter ever recorded (up to that time) in Iowa history. Not exactly the easiest introduction to producing, but just the sort of obstacle-laden path that brings out the best in Taurus.

## Audrey Hepburn (May 4, 1929)

Fragile gamines don't necessarily come to mind when one thinks about the robust physical stereotype usually associated with Taurus. However, Audrey Hepburn's delicacy was only skin (and bone) deep. A class act on screen and off, she was as comfortable cradling sick children as part of her duties for UNICEF as she was romancing the likes of Rex Harrison, Cary Grant and Peter O'Toole. Though she only made about twenty films in her entire career, her impact was extraordinary and unforgettable, whether she was running through Rome with Gregory Peck in "Roman Holiday;" sparring with Harrison in "My Fair Lady;" or dancing with Fred Astaire in "Funny Face." Movies like "Breakfast at Tiffany's" and "Sabrina" shaped her legacy and spawned a generation of young girls who grew up wanting to be sophisticated like Audrey Hepburn. She was, and still remains, unique.

**Suggested Rental:** "Robin and Marian" (1975)
In this haunting elegy for aging legends, Sean Connery plays a grizzled Robin Hood, twenty years after his merry days in Sherwood and newly returned from the grueling Crusades. Hepburn is his Maid Marian, now cloistered from the secular world as a Mother Superior in a convent. Nicol Williamson is a stalwart Little John, while Robert Shaw contributes a fine turn as the still-villainous-after-all-these-years Sheriff of Nottingham. The film is directed by Richard Lester, who did "Help" and "A Hard Day's Night," so there are vestiges of an antic, post-Carnaby Street humor. But the essential tone is autumnal and slightly melancholy, as if we can all feel the slight ache in Robin's joints or Marian's modest embarrassment at the few wisps of gray in her hair. The appeal for Taureans is a kind of beyond-youth, beyond-time steadfastness — two people made for each other in life and in death.

**Taurus Moment:** Hepburn hadn't made a movie in eight years. What surprised screenwriter James Goldman was that she would choose a role like this for her comeback. When the film was finished shooting, he mused in an interview, "It would be interesting to know why Marian appealed to Audrey. In her former roles, she always played the innocent woman who had been swept up by circumstances. . . . Marian is a strong woman with a determined will and yet impulsively emotional – it's not what one expects of Audrey's image." It is, however, what one expects from a true-blue Taurus.

## Michelle Pfeiffer (April 29, 1957)

Like Audrey Hepburn, Michelle Pfeiffer doesn't fit the physical stereotype of the robust Taurean. But, again like Hepburn, there's far more to her than meets – and pleases – the eye. She could've had a reasonably healthy career as a decorative blonde; she demonstrated her ability to play that role in "Scarface" opposite Al Pacino. Instead, she opted for a range of parts: the scene-stealing Catwoman in "Batman Returns;" the sexy torch signer who burned that baby grand in "The Fabulous Baker Boys;" an angry, bitter farmer's daughter in "A Thousand Acres;" a lonely, seen-it-all waitress in "Frankie and Johnny;" a worldly sophisticate in "The Age of Innocence;" a kick-ass teacher in "Dangerous Minds;" and a gum-snapping Mafia widow in "Married to the Mob." She has intelligence, versatility and a Taurean's stubborn drive. And cheekbones to die for.

**Suggested Rental:** "Ladyhawke" (1985)
Pfeiffer costars with Rutger Hauer in this spellbinding movie about spellbound lovers. Hauer is the bold knight on a black steed who travels only by day, accompanied by a hawk;

Pfeifer is the fair lady in a black cape who travels only at night, accompanied by a wolf. As anyone who knows what shape King Arthur's table was can probably guess, the pair are victims of an evil enchantment. The only one who can help is a thief (a young Matthew Broderick) who'd really rather not. With their matching blue eyes and matchless profiles, the two stars are perfectly cast as lovers out of legend, and their unwavering devotion to each other provides the Taurean spin. Director Richard Donner ("Lethal Weapon") makes this a medieval romance told with Victorian vigor, a full-gallop kind of film that mixes the primitive power of a Frazetta drawing with the mystery of an illuminated manuscript.

**Taurus Moment:** When Donner was casting the film, he didn't have time to meet Pfeiffer in person for a screen test, so he asked that she send a videotape. She later recalled that, at first, "my ego got really bent out of shape. I had many questions to ask Donner that now I wouldn't get answered." Then, her Taurus comon-sense side took over. She turned the taped test into an opportunity. She bought a parakeet at a pet shop and let it do half the test. Not a bad idea for a role in which you spend half your screen time as a hawk.

### Jack Nicholson (April 22, 1937)

He can be Smilin' Jack or Psycho Jack. Mostly, he's Jack the Nimble, the zillionaire Joker who worked his way up from Roger Corman's B-movie basement to the top of Hollywood's very short A-list. Jack Nicholson isn't just a great actor — as we've seen in everything from "Easy Rider" and "One Flew Over the Cukoo's Nest," to "The Shining" and "As Good as It Gets" — he's a great Jack Nicholson. Nobody does it better. The killer smile. The quizzical eyebrows. The bad-boy lovability. He's also something of a great conundrum — an anti-establish-ment icon who's spent most of his adult life enjoying the rewards of the establishment. True to his Taurean roots, Nicholson loves the good life — multiple homes, expensive cars, an extensive staff. He's the outsider as insider, our one and only desperado-hedonist. One thing is always clear: It's good to be Jack.

**Suggested Rental:** "Terms of Endearment" (1983)
This movie has got Taurus stamped all over it. Not just in its on-camera characters who manifest such Taurean traits as steadfastness, materialism, and willful stubbornness, but in its very Taurean off-camera pedigree. It was directed by a Taurus (James L. Brooks) and stars three Tauruses (Nicholson, Debra Winger and Shirley Maclaine), and they all won Oscars. The movie demands to be taken on its own terms — and those terms change as it goes along. Smart, funny, emotionally devastating, it starts out like the best "Mary Tyler Moore" episode ever (Brooks did that show, too) and then, ever so slowly, becomes far richer and more real. It spans thirty years in a mother-daughter relationship (MacLaine and Debra Winger), adding on the different peo-ple who also become important to them. The stand-out is Nicholson, in the supporting but pivotal role of the wom-anizing astronaut-next-door.

**Taurus Moment:** Nicholson's character, Garrett Breedlove, didn't exist in Larry McMurtry's novel. It was created by Brooks as both a composite of Aurora's (MacLaine's) lovers and as a much-needed counterpoint to a female-dominated story. At first, no one thought a star of Nicholson's calibre woud consider a supporting role — make that, a *third*-billed supporting role. But like most Taureans, he knew that you can be in second place and still be first rate. So he took the part — and took home his second Oscar.

## MOVIES "BORN" UNDER TAURUS

WUTHERING HEIGHTS
GOODBYE MR. CHIPS
HEATHERS
FIELD OF DREAMS
MIAMI BLUES
Q & A
WHAT ABOUT BOB
A MIDNIGHT CLEAR
DAVE
LOST IN YONKERS

CROOKLYN
THE CROW
MAVERICK
WHILE YOU WERE SLEEPING
FORGET PARIS
A LITTLE PRINCESS
LAST DANCE
THE GREAT WHITE HYPE
TWISTER
AUSTIN POWERS

## OTHER FAMOUS TAURUSES

*Ryan O'Neal*

Charles Grodin (1935)
Anthony Quinn (1916)
Edwin S. Porter (1870)

**APRIL 22**
Sheryl Lee (1967)
Chris Makepeace (1964)
Catherine Mary Stewart
  (1959)
Marilyn Chambers (1954)
Joseph Bottoms (1954)
John Waters (1946)
Jack Nicholson (1937)
Glen Campbell (1936)
Eddie Albert (1908)

**APRIL 20**
Crispin Glover (1964)
Veronica Cartwright (1950)
Jessica Lange (1949)
Ryan O'Neal (1941)
James Gammon (1940)
Nina Foch (1924)

**APRIL 21**
Andie MacDowell (1958)
Steve Dorff (1949)
Patti Lupone (1949)
Claire Denis (1948)

**APRIL 23**
Craig Sheffer (1960)
Jan Hooks (1957)
James Russo (1953)

Blair Brown (1948)
Sandra Dee (1942)
Shirley Temple (1928)
Janet Blair (1921)
Basil Sydney (1894)
Frank Borzage (1893)

**APRIL 24**
Michael O'Keefe (1955)
Eric Bogosian (1953)
Barbra Streisand (1942)
Jill Ireland (1936)
Shirley MacLaine (1934)
William Castle (1914)

**APRIL 25**
Hank Azaria (1964)
Talia Shire (1946)
Bertrand Tavernier (1941)

**APRIL 26**
Jackie Chan (1961)
Giancarlo Esposito (1958)
Bobby Rydell (1942)
Carol Burnett (1933)
Jean Vigo (1905)
Douglas Sirk (1900)
Anita Loos (1893)
Edgar Kennedy (1890)
William Desmond Taylor (1877)

**APRIL 27**
Sandy Dennis (1937)
Anouk Aimee (1932)
Jack Klugman (1922)

**APRIL 28**
Mary McDonnell (1952)
Bruno Kirby (1949)
Ann-Margret (1941)
Carolyn Jones (1929)
Lionel Barrymore (1878)

*Uma Thurman*

**APRIL 29**
Uma Thurman (1970)
Michelle Pfeiffer (1957)
Daniel Day-Lewis (1957)
Jerry Seinfeld (1955)
Kate Mulgrew (1955)
Phillip Noyce (1950)
Richard Lynch (1936)
Lane Smith (1936)
Irving Kershner (1923)
Celeste Holm (1919)
Tom Ewell (1909)
Fred Zinneman (1907)
Hope Emerson (1897)

**APRIL 30**
Kirsten Dunst (1982)
Lars Von Trier (1956)
Perry King (1948)
Bill Plympton (1946)
Jill Clayburgh (1944)
Burt Young (1940)

Willie Nelson (1933)
Cloris Leachman (1926)
Eve Arden (1912)

**MAY 1**
Danielle Darrieux (1917)
Glenn Ford (1916)
Henry Kostner (1905)
Joan Hackett (1938)

**MAY 2**
Theodore Bikel (1924)
Satyajit Ray (1921)
Brian Aherne (1902)

**MAY 3**
Bobby Driscoll (1937)
Mary Astor (1906)
Bing Crosby (1903)
Walter Slezak (1902)
Beulah Bondi (1892)

**MAY 4**
Paul Gleason (1944)
Audrey Hepburn (1929)
Eric Sykes (1923)
Howard Da Silva (1909)
Luther Adler (1903)

**MAY 5**
Richard E. Grant (1957)
Roger Rees (1941)
Jean-Pierre Leaud (1944)
John Rhys-Davies (1944)
Michael Palin (1943)
Lance Henrikson (1940)

Michael Murphy (1938)
Jerzy Skolimowski (1938)
Alice Faye (1915)
Tyrone Power (1914)

**MAY 6**
Dana Hill (1964)
Lori Singer (1962)
George Clooney (1961)
Anne Parillaud (1960)
Russ Hunter (1921)
Orson Welles (1915)
Stewart Granger (1913)
Max Ophuls (1902)
Rudolph Valentino (1895)

**MAY 7**
Traci Lords (1968)
Amy Heckerling (1955)
David Keith (1954)
John Irvin (1940)
Anne Baxter (1923)
Darren McGaven (1922)
David Tomlinson (1917)
Val Lewton (1904)
Gary Cooper (1901)
George "Gabby" Hayes (1885)

**MAY 8**
Rick Nelson (1940)
Don Rickles (1926)
Lex Baxter (1919)
Roberto Rossellini (1906)
Fernandel (1903)

**MAY 9**
Candice Bergen (1946)
James L. Brooks (1940)
Albert Finney (1936)
Glenda Jackson (1936)
Fuzzy Knight (1901)
Richard Barthelmess (1895)

**MAY 10**
Cary Guffey (1972)
Meg Foster (1948)
Jim Abrahams (1949)
Marie-France Pisler (1944)
Ettore Scola (1931)
David O. Selznick (1902)
Fred Astaire (1899)
Clarence Brown (1890)
Mae Murray (1889)

**MAY 11**
Natasha Richardson (1963)
Denver Pyle (1920)
Phil Silvers (1912)
Margaret Rutherford (1892)

**MAY 12**
Samantha Mathis (1970)
Stephen Baldwin (1966)
Emilio Estevez (1962)
Kim Greist (1958)
Gabriel Byrne (1950)
Lindsay Crouse (1948)
Susan Hampshire (1938)
Millie Perkins (1938)
Katharine Hepburn (1907)

**MAY 13**
Harvey Keitel (1941)
Senta Berger (1941)
Herbert Ross (1927)
Bea Arthur (1923)
Brad Dexter (1917)

**MAY 14**
Tim Roth (1961)
Robert Zemeckis (1952)
David Byrne (1952)
George Lucas (1944)

**MAY 15**
Chazz Palminteri (1952)
Lainie Kazan (1942)
Joseph Wiseman (1927)
Constance Cummings (1910)
James Mason (1906)
Joseph Cotten (1905)

*Pierce Brosnan*

**MAY 16**
Tori Spelling (1973)
Janet Jackson (1966)
Mare Winningham (1959)
Debra Winger (1955)
Pierce Brosnan (1953)
Harry Carey Jr. (1921)
Margaret Sullavan (1911)

Henry Fonda (1905)

**MAY 17**
Bill Paxton (1955)
Dennis Hopper (1936)
Dennis Potter (1935)
Jean Gabin (1904)

**MAY 18**
Chow Yun-Fat (1955)
Miriam Margolyes (1941)
Robert Morse (1931)
James Donald (1917)
Richard Brooks (1912)
Frank Capra (1897)
Enzio Pinza (1892)

**MAY 19**
Grace Jones (1948)
Nora Ephron (1941)
James Fox (1939)
Nancy Kwan (1939)

*Cher*

**MAY 20**
Tony Goldwyn (1960)
Bronson Pinchot (1959)
Dave Thomas (1949)
Jon Amiel (1948)
Cher (1946)
Anthony Zerbe (1936)
Danny Aiello (1933)

# GEMINI

## MAY 21 — JUNE 20

Lively, attention-loving Geminis are drawn to the limelight like moths to a flame. They are the zodiac's master salesmen, always ready with a fast line or a good quip. Think of Robert Preston (June 8) as Professor Harold Hill in "The Music Man" and you've got a pretty good idea of the type.

But Geminis can't help it. Their minds are always whirring in mental overdrive. On the upside, that means they're spontaneous, clever and perceptive. On the downside, they can be scattered, unreliable and egocentric. Marilyn Monroe was a Gemini. So, I'll bet, is Peter Pan — though probably not the Disney version.

Naturally, that gift for gab and charged mental energy serve them well in Hollywood, where first impressions are all-important (and Geminis make first-rate first impressions) and the ability to sell yourself isn't just a plus but a necessity.

The bottom line on Geminis is that they're a blast to be

around, *when* they're around, that is. Like the born social butterflies they are, they flit from one thing to another, going wherever their restless, curious natures take them. Dean Martin, Joan Collins, Michael J. Fox, Bob Hope, Helen Hunt and Tim Allen are all Geminis. They're also all top-of-the-class chatty flirts when they want to be. But strong, silent types, like John Wayne and Clint Eastwood, also were born under the sign of the twins. That's the Gemini trick: changeable, versatile and mercurial. What you see with a Gemini isn't always what you get.

The Gemini movie-lover is naturally drawn to movies about twins. Try "Dead Ringers" (double Jeremy Irons), "The Parent Trap" (double Hayley Mills) and "Start the Revolution without Me" (mismatched twins Donald Sutherland and Gene Wilder). Also, "The Krays" and — why not? — any of the "Dr. Jekyll and Mr. Hyde" movies. They also like mentally stimulating puzzles — light-hearted ones like "Murder on the Orient Express" or darker ones like "Body Heat." Smart, astringent comedies work well, too. Check out Preston Sturges or Billy Wilder in the classics section. And remember, Geminis are easily bored. So leave the moody stuff to Scorpio and the do-gooder stuff to Aquarius.

## FIVE SUGGESTED RENTALS

### "Who Framed Roger Rabbit" (1988)

Long before Robert Zemeckis Gump-ed Tom Hanks in and out of history, he treated movie-lovers to this dazzling special-effects extravaganza. Like an animated "Around the World in 80 Days," the picture is littered with cameo appearances by cartoon greats. Daffy and Donald play a ducky piano duet. Bugs and Mickey share a magical moment of free fall. The movie is built around the sort of spontaneous "cool-idea!" that Geminis love. It is set in '40s Hollywood, in a world where pen-and-ink characters co-exist with flesh-and-blood counterparts. The cartoons report to the studio for work, and then they go home to their anything-can-happen Technicolor ghetto, Toontown. The story follows a seedy private investigator (the marvelous Bob Hoskins), who is hired by a mogul to find out what's bugging his star animated bunny, Roger (a true bouncing-off-the-wall Gemini). One clue: his sultry toon wife, Jessica (voice by Kathleen Turner), may be fooling around.

### "Bob Roberts" (1992)

A winner by a landslide. Written and directed by Tim Robbins, this clever political satire charts the irresistable rise of an image-savvy folksinger (Robbins) who calls himself a "rebel conservative." (media double-talk for somewhere right of Genghis Khan). Framed as a documentary being filmed by the BBC, the picture follows Roberts in his race for the Senate against a liberal incumbent (novelist Gore Vidal!). Geminis will love how sardonically observant the movie is. Robbins can be obvious, but he pretty much hits his targets dead-on, from Roberts' smooth, sound-bite ideology and neofascist sing-alongs ("Times Are Changin' Back" goes one title) to the compliant photo-op coverage provided by happy-faced anchors. It's a caustic cautionary tale that leaves a lingering bit of disquiet: is this parody or prophecy?

### "Swimming to Cambodia" (1987)

No one can string words together like a Gemini on a roll, and Spalding Gray (born June 5) can outtalk ninety percent of his Twin colleagues. This, his first monologue/movie, touches on everything from Bangkok brothels and bit parts in big movies, to the Khymer Rouge and what killed Marilyn Monroe. The central thread is Gray's experience acting in "The Killing Fields" which he uses as a launching pad for ruminations on late-night movie shoots, lewd Thai sex shows, actors' egos and despots' evils. A riveting storyteller with the free-association reflexes of a less bitter Lenny Bruce, Gray turns talk into art. Translation: He's Gemini in a nutshell. Aided and abetted by director Jonathan Demme, Gray gives us a state-of-the-performance-art confessional about the state of the world and, more important (for him), the state of Spalding Gray.

## "White Mischief" (1988)

A kind of Noel Coward nastiness permeates this tale of cutting up among the British upper crust in Kenya during the '40s. Based on true events, it's a saga of sex and murder among the rich and, eventually, infamous. The major players: wealthy old Sir Jock Broughton (Joss Ackland); his predatory trophy wife, Diana (Greta Scacchi); and Joss Erroll (Charles Dance), a notorious ladies' man who's long on titles but short on cash. The ensuing scandal even knocked Hitler off the front page as it focused attention on the aristocratic rot infecting these pampered ex-patriates in paradise. Basically, it's a movie about people with absolutely no redeeming social value, unless you count their social status. Gemini's more archly superficial side will be enraptured by — and maybe identify with — this sinfully delicious tea-danse macabre.

## "The King of Comedy" (1983)

Movies don't come much smarter than Martin Scorsese's brilliantly daring cult classic. The hollow men are Jerry Langford (Jerry Lewis), a big-time talk-show host, and Rupert Pupkin (Robert De Niro), a small-time nobody who desperately wants to deliver a stand-up routine on Jerry's show. The movie flirts with a number of themes: obsession with celebrity, celebrity stalkers, the media's message/massage and the dark seeds sown by rejection. Like a time bomb that refuses to go off, it's a courageous and complex work, less funny "ha-ha" as funny "uh-oh." De Niro and Sandra Bernhard, his partner-in-obsessiveness, are misfit twins (twins??) — high-strung, egocentric, always going off on tangents as they close in on the object of their conflicted affections (Lewis). Ultimately,

Scorsese's film reminds us not of the banality of evil, but of the evil of banality.

## SIX TALENTED GEMINIS

### Annette Bening (May 29, 1958)

When Annette Bening was cast opposite Warren Beatty in "Bugsy," the gossip-mongers immediately speculated whether she'd become his next conquest. Guess who conquested who? Bening ended up Mrs. Beatty, hooking the legendarily unhookable star. That − and their three children − has slowed down her career a bit. Still, she's managed to work in "The American President," "Love Affair" and "Richard III." Hardly similar movies. Neither were the ones she made pre-Warren: "Valmont," "The Great Outdoors," "The Grifters," "Regarding Henry" and "Guilty by Suspicion." About the only thing Bening can't do − and this is her Gemini side coming out − is play dumb. All her characters are alert, mentally agile and, most of all, adaptable. She's been plenty adaptable off screen as well; she was supposed to play Catwoman in "Batman Returns," but was otherwise engaged: having Beatty's baby.

**Suggested rental:** "The Grifters" (1990)
Based on Jim Thompson's noir cult novel, Stephen Frears's smashing film is exhilarating, sordid and as uncompromising as a rigged shell game. The movie is all angles, and I don't mean camera placement. The focus is on a trio of crafty con-artists: Anjelica Huston, who places bets for a much-feared mobster; her son, John Cusack, who specializes in penny-ante scams; and Bening, Cusack's girlfriend, a sharp-witted dish who comes on like a ditz but is nobody's fool. The plot comes down to a tug-of-war between the two women, both cut from the same crooked cloth, over the less lethal Cusack.

Geminis will love the the way Frears and his cast have captured an insular netherworld of larcenous nuance and sleazy panache, bolstered by a sly gallows humor. Pitch-dark and pitch-perfect, the film is a nasty, knowing celebration of the fast-talkers of the world.

**Gemini Moment:** Bening's movie, "Valmont" was the "twin," so to speak of "Dangerous Liaisons." That is, they were based on the same story, with Bening playing the same role Glenn Close played in "Liaisons," which, coincidentally, was directed by Frears who first met Bening when he asked her to audition for *that* movie. He ended up not using her, but she made enough of an impression to get the call for "The Grifters," beating out the director's original choice, Geena Davis.

### Laurence Olivier (May 22, 1907)

There is no better example of Gemini's unmatchable talent for silver-tongued deviltry than the magnificent Olivier, who is not only one of the greatest actors of this century but, arguably, one of the greatest actors *ever.* Olivier could do it all: the spidery evil of "Richard III;" the grand romantic passion of "Wuthering Heights;" the haughty manipulations of "Spartacus;" the for-God-and-country heroism of "Henry V;" the seedy pathos of "The Entertainer;" the conflicted intelligence of "Hamlet;" and the hammy villainy of "Marathon Man." A Gemini through and through, he was vain, mercurial and a shameless flirt (though he preferred to seduce audiences). The story goes that when he and Dustin Hoffman were doing "Marathon Man," a scene called for them both to be out of breath. Hoffman ran around Central Park until he was exhausted and then asked his costar how he prepared. Olivier replied, "I pretend." Gemini to the bone.

**Suggested Rental:** "Sleuth" (1972)

Mind games galore as Olivier and Michael Caine act the bejesus out of Anthony Shaffer's stylish bit of stage trickery. Not surprisingly, they both earned Oscar nominations for their work. Olivier is a wealthy, famous mystery writer who discovers that his much younger neighbor (Caine) is having an affair with his wife. Less out of hurt feelings than hurt pride (he cannot stand being a cuckold), he concocts a real-life murder plot that has some surprising results. The movie is clever and showy – very much to Gemini's taste – and chock full of puzzles, tricks and dress-up games (more Gemini territory). Ultimately, it's a heck of a cat-and-mouse game played out by two very smart cats. And even if you've seen it before and know what twists are coming, the sheer joy the actors take in their duel of wits makes a second viewing all the more pleasurable.

**Gemini Moment:** The movie's theme of don't-believe-what-you-see is set immediately in the opening credits. Listed among the cast is Margo Channing, the actress character played by Bette Davis in "All About Eve," which was directed by Joseph Mankiewicz who also directed – that's right – "Sleuth." Clever, clever, *clever.*

## Liam Neeson (June 7, 1952)

He has the matinee-idol looks, the leading-man charisma and, just to tie the whole package together, that irresistable Irish accent. No wonder he dated everyone from Barbra Streisand to Helen Mirren before marrying Natasha Richardson. Yet it took Liam Neeson years of hard work to make it to Hollywood's A-list. Not that he didn't do good movies – "The Good Mother," "Darkman," "Husbands and Wives" and "Excalibur," to name a few – but none of them seemed to give him that extra push. Then along came "Schindler's List" and everything changed.

Gemini's blarney side comes easily to Neeson, yet he employs it in unexpected ways, like Schindler's bon-vivant buoyancy or the quiet determination of his doctor character in "Nell" or in the reluctant rabble-rousing of "Rob Roy." Neeson has Gemini's warmth, alertness and intuition. He's a character actor disguised as a hunk.

**Suggested Rental:** "Michael Collins" (1996)
The short turbulent life of Michael Collins (Neeson), the Irish revolutionary who freed the southern part of his country from 700 years of British rule, and, more controversially, invented modern urban-guerila tactics, is given the David Lean treatment (i.e., impassioned, intelligent, sweeping) by director Neil Jordan. The supporting cast ranges from Alan Rickman (chilly and connniving) to Julia Roberts (very pretty, but not sure what to do with her underwritten role) to handsome Aidan Quinn as Collins's best friend and rival for Roberts's affections. Neeson's masterful portrait of Collins is an uncanny evocation of everything Gemini about him. He gives us a complex, mercurial figure — swaggering one minute, conscience-stricken the next, as affable as he is ruthless. Though there were protests over the film's overall accuracy, it's a bold, powerful work that stands as tall as its hero.

**Gemini Moment:** Twinned ideas are about as comon in Hollywood as swimming pools, and wouldn't you know it, just when Jordan and Neeson were getting close to a green light on a dream that had taken them years to pull together, Kevin Costner announced *he* had a new project in mind: the story of this Irish guy, Michael Collins. But by 1995, Costner was busy with other things and Neeson and Jordan's stars had risen enough for them to prevail.

## Morgan Freeman (June 1, 1937)

Morgan Freeman is one of those actors who commands instant respect. Whether he's playing a chauffeur in "Driving Miss Daisy," an abolitionist in "Amistad" or a prison inmate in "The Shawshank Redemption," there's something regal about him. No wonder Public Theatre director Joe Papp said he "looked like a king." Yet, for almost twenty years, Freeman was royally underemployed. The steadiest work he could find was on TV, playing the rappin' hippie, Easy Reader, on "The Electric Company." But at age fifty, he was "discovered" when Pauline Kael began her review of the movie "Street Smart" with the question, "Is Morgan Freeman the greatest actor in America today?" On the surface, Freeman seems too calm, too centered to be a Gemini. But his Gemini changeability is channeled into his work. He hides in plain sight by disappearing into his characters.

**Suggested Rental:** "Street Smart" (1987)

The movie was supposed to focus on Christopher Reeve, who was making one of his periodic attempts to shake his Superman image. He plays an ambitious New York reporter who fakes a story about a street pimp with disastrous results. However, Freeman stole the picture with his riveting performance as the pimp, Fast Black. But he wasn't your standard TV-edition pimp dressed in gold chains and velvet. He was smart, intuitive, charming and evil. In one harrowing scene, he threatens one of his whores (Kathy Baker) with a pair of scissors and asks her which of her eyes she'd prefer to lose. The movie is the sort of fascinating, off-beat work that barely stayed in the theaters because the studios didn't know what to do with it; they just wanted a straightforward action flick. Which is another way of saying that, like some Geminis, "Street Smart" was too smart for its own good.

**Gemini Moment:** For most of us, things happen in threes. But for those born under the sign of the Twins, they often happen in twos. For instance, the very same week that "Street Smart" opened in movie theaters, "Driving Miss Daisy" opened Off-Broadway. And it was that one-two punch that gave Freeman his breakthrough.

## Bob Hope (May 29, 1903)

Bob Hope has traveled down many roads during his film career. But the most important road was the one that took him to Hollywood. England-born and Cleveland-raised, Hope transformed himself into a quintessential American funny man, a brash fast-talker (hello, Gemini) who could, at the drop of a cue card, come up with a well-timed quip about a political candidate, an Oscar hopeful or Bing Crosby. His screen persona was a canny mix of cowardice and bluster, of preening pseudonarcissism and duck-and-cover insecurities (generally expressed by one of his trademark wisecracks). In many ways, Hope is a pure expresssion of a Gemini comedian – not that he isn't graceful, but unlike Chaplin, the Marx Brothers or, more recently, Jim Carrey, his humor is almost entirely verbal. He hasn't shut up for more than half a century, proving that where there's Hope, there's liveliness. And laughs.

**Suggested Rental:** "The Road to Morocco" (1942)
This was Hope and Crosby's third road trip together and by the time they headed for Morocco (as the song lyric goes, "Like Webster's dictionary, we're Morocco-bound"), the series' formula had pretty well been established. The plot remains inconsequential: they rescue a beautiful princess (Dorothy Lamour) from a villainous sheik (Anthony Quinn). But the movie's tone – and this is what will appeal to flip, hip Geminis – is more knowing and self-referential. Early in the movie when they're

stranded in the desert, Hope says, "Lay you eight to five we meet Dorothy Lamour." Later on, when things aren't looking too good for the pair, Hope notes reassuringly, "Paramount will protect us. We're signed for four more years." One scene to look for is their close encounter with a camel, an ill-tempered creature that spits in Hope's face. Note that he staggers off-camera while Crosby cracks up. The spit was ad-libbed.

**Gemini Moment:** Pairs play a huge part in Gemini lives, and the pairing of Hope and Crosby in the "Road" series wasn't as fated as it might seem. The first picture, "The Road to Singapore," was originally written for George Burns and Gracie Allen. When that didn't work out, somebody came up with Fred MacMurray and Jack Oakie. Luckily, *that* didn't pan out either. So some anonymous studio stooge/genius suggested Hope and Crosby. And the rest is . . .

## Nicole Kidman (June 20, 1967)

For a long time, even her startling red mane and drop-dead looks couldn't offset Nicole Kidman's primary identity problem. Namely, as far as Hollywood and the rest of the world were concerned, she was, first and foremost, Mrs. Tom Cruise. Some of that was self-inflicted, as the two met while making "Days of Thunder," then costarred in "Far and Away" and spent more than a year in England working on Stanley Kubrick's "Eyes Wide Open." But her Gemini need for attention helped push her out of her husband's shadow. That and roles in movies like "Malice," "The Peacemaker," "Portrait of a Lady," "Batman Forever" and, most important, "To Die For." Her translucent skin and sky-blue eyes reflect her air-sign origins. So does her airy sense of humor about her sudden standing as a Hollywood insider simply because of her husband's star status. She's having a good time, and it shows.

**Suggested Rental:** "To Die For" (1995)
Director Gus Van Sant takes a wickedly comic look at TV-spawned celebrity obsession. Kidman plays Suzanne Stone, a psychopathic, Jane Pauley wannabe stuck as a weathergirl at a nowhere cable station. The plot kicks in when Kidman decides one impediment to her video dreams is her husband (Matt Dillon) and his cozy vision of a Happy Meal future together. Adapted by Buck Henry from Joyce Maynard's book (which was based on a real small-town scandal), the picture is a hilarious study of strawberry-blonde ambition as well as a blackly humorous cautionary tale of what can happen in a nation of soft-heads and "Hard Copy." As flakily flirtatious as its very Gemini heroine, the film catches a startling moment in our nation's Jerry Springer-ized psyche. Working her way through the barrage of reporters after certain events, Kidman sparkles like a '90s Norma Desmond. She's ready for her close-up, Mr. Bochco.

**Gemini Moment:** Kidman was not the director's first choice, but when Meg Ryan bowed out, Kidman went after the part with a determination worthy of her character. The key, she figured, was the TV-obsession along with the off-center determination. Not only did she call up Van Sant and insist that it was her destiny to play the role (something Suzanne herself might've done), but she concentrated, Gemini-like, on the level of celeb attention that Suzanne craved. Locking herself in a hotel room for three days, she absorbed all the talk shows she could find and even subjected herself to regular doses of the Home Shopping Network.

## MOVIES "BORN" AS GEMINIS

| | |
|---|---|
| YOUNG MR. LINCOLN | TOTAL RECALL |
| EARTH GIRLS ARE EASY | DICK TRACY |
| DEAD POETS SOCIETY | THELMA AND LOUISE |

SOAP DISH
CITY SLICKERS
ROBIN HOOD: PRINCE OF
  THIEVES
FAR AND AWAY
SISTER ACT
BATMAN RETURNS
HOT SHOTS
WHAT'S LOVE GOT TO DO

WITH IT
SPEED
BRAVEHEART
BRIDGES OF MADISON
  COUNTY
POCOHANTAS
THE LOST WORLD
MY BEST FRIEND'S WEDDING

## OTHER FAMOUS GEMINIS

**MAY 21**
Fairuza Balk (1974)
Nick Cassavetes (1959)
Judge Reinhold (1956)
Mr. T (1952)
Joan Collins (1933)
Kay Kendall (1927)
Raymond Burr (1917)
Robert Montgomery (1904)

**MAY 22**
Alison Eastwood (1972)
Paul Winfield (1941)
Michael Sarrazin (1940)
Susan Strasberg (1938)
Richard Benjamin (1938)
Michael Constantine (1927)
Laurence Olivier (1907)

**MAY 23**
Helena Bonham Carter (1966)
Nigel Davenport (1928)
Betty Garrett (1919)

John Payne (1912)
Douglas Fairbanks (1883)

**MAY 24**
Alfred Molina (1953)
Priscilla Presley (1945)
Bob Dylan (1941)
Gary Burghoff (1940)
Tommy Chong (1938)
Lilli Palmer (1914)

**MAY 25**
Justin Henry (1971)
Anne Heche (1969)
Mike Myers (1963)
Bob Goldthwait (1962)
Frank Oz (1944)
Jeanne Crain (1925)
Claude Akins (1918)

**MAY 26**
Travis Fine (1967)
Pam Grier (1949)

Alec McCowen (1925)
James Arness (1923)
Peter Cushing (1913)
Robert Morley (1908)
John Wayne (1907)
Norma Talmadge (1895)
Al Jolson (1886)

**MAY 27**
Louis Gossett Jr. (1936)
Lee Meriweather (1935)
Christopher Lee (1922)
Willie Best (1913)
Vincent Price (1911)

**MAY 28**
Chiara Mastroianni (1972)
Sondra Locke (1947)
Carroll Baker (1931)
Martha Vickers (1925)

**MAY 29**
Rupert Everett (1959)
Annette Bening (1958)
Nick Mancuso (1948)
Helmut Berger (1944)
Kevin Conway (1942)
Bob Hope (1903)
Josef Von Sternberg (1894)

**MAY 30**
Colm Meaney (1953)
Stephen Tablowsky (1951)
Michael J. Pollard (1939)
Keir Dullea (1936)
Franklin J. Schaffner (1920)

Hugh Griffith (1912)
Mel Blanc (1908)
Stepin Fetchit (1902)
Irving Thalberg (1899)
Howard Hawks (1896)

*Clint Eastwood*

**MAY 31**
Sandrine Bonnaire (1967)
Brooke Shields (1965)
Lea Thompson (1961)
Tom Berenger (1950)
Rainer Werner Fassbinder
   (1945)
Jim Hutton (1934)
Clint Eastwood (1930)
Denholm Elliott (1922)
Don Ameche (1908)

*Marilyn Monroe*

**JUNE 1**
Jonathan Pryce (1947)
Rene Auberjonois (1940)
Cleavon Little (1939)

Morgan Freeman (1947)
Pat Boone (1934)
Edward Woodward (1930)
Andy Griffith (1926)
Marilyn Monroe (1926)
Robert Newton (1905)

**JUNE 2**
Joanna Gleason (1950)
Jon Peters (1945)
Stacy Keach (1941)
Sally Kellerman (1937)
Milo O'Shea (1926)
Johnny Weismuller (1904)
Hedda Hopper (1890)

**JUNE 3**
Colleen Dewhurst (1926)
Tony Curtis (1925)
Alain Resnais (1922)
Leo Gorcy (1926)
Paulette Godard (1911)
Maurice Evans (1901)

**JUNE 4**
Noah Wylie (1971)
Michelle Phillips (1944)
Bruce Dern (1936)
Dennis Weaver (1924)
Rosalind Russell (1908)

**JUNE 5**
Mark Wahlberg (1971)
Spalding Gray (1941)
Robert Lansing (1929)
Jacques Demy (1931)

Tony Richardson (1928)
William Boyd (1898)

**JUNE 6**
Amanda Pays (1959)
Sandra Bernhard (1955)
Harvey Fierstein (1954)
Lasse Halstrom (1946)
Billie Whitelaw (1932)
Maria Montez (1917)

**JUNE 7**
Prince (1958)
Liam Neeson (1952)
Virginia McKenna (1931)
James Ivory (1928)
Dolores Gray (1924)
Jessica Tandy (1909)

**JUNE 8**
Keenan Ivory Wayans (1958)
Griffin Dunne (1955)
Kathy Baker (1947)
Bernie Casey (1939)
James Darren (1936)
Joan Rivers (1933)
Bo Widerberg (1930)
Alexis Smith (1921)
Robert Preston (1918)

*Johnny Depp*

**JUNE 9**
Natalie Portman (1981)
Johnny Depp (1963)
Michael J. Fox (1961)

**JUNE 10**
Vincent Perez (1965)
Elizabeth Hurly (1965)
Elisabeth Shue (1963)
Gina Gershon (1962)
Lionel Jeffries (1926)
Judy Garland (1922)
Robert Cummings (1908)
Hattie McDaniel (1895)
Sessue Hayakawa (1890)

**JUNE 11**
Adrienne Barbeau (1945)
Chad Everett (1936)
Gene Wilder (1935)
Richard Todd (1919)
Carmine Coppola (1910)
Wesley Ruggles (1889)
Max Schreck (1879)

**JUNE 12**
Ally Sheedy (1962)
Vic Damone (1928)
Samuel Z. Arkoff (1918)
Irwin Allen (1916)

**JUNE 13**
Mary-Kate and Ashley Olsen (1986)
Tim Allen (1953)
Richard Thomas (1951)

Simon Callow (1949)
Paul Lynde (1926)
Ben Johnson (1918)
Mary Wickes (1916)
Basil Rathbone (1892)

**JUNE 14**
Will Patton (1954)
Anthony Sher (1949)
Gene Barry (1921)
Dorothy McGuire (1918)
Burl Ives (1909)
Cliff Edwards (1895)

*Helen Hunt*

**JUNE 15**
Ice Cube (1969)
Courteney Cox (1964)
Helen Hunt (1963)
Polly Draper (1956)
Julie Hagerty (1955)
Jim Belushi (1954)
Jim Varney (1950)
Malcolm McDowell (1943)
Claude Brasseur (1936)
Lash La Rue (1917)
Harry Langdon (1884)

**JUNE 16**
Lukas Haas (1976)

# GEMINI

Tupac Shakur (1971)
Laurie Metcalf (1955)
Joan Van Ark (1943)
Vilmos Zsigmond (1930)
Jack Albertson (1907)
Stan Laurel (1890)

## JUNE 17
Greg Kinnear (1963)
Ken Loach (1936)
Dean Martin (1917)
Ralph Bellamy (1904)

## JUNE 18
Isabella Rossellini (1952)
Carol Kane (1952)
Paul McCartney (1942)
Richard Boone (1917)
E. G. Marshall (1914)
Keye Luke (1904)
Jeanette MacDonald (1903)
Blanche Sweet (1898)

## JUNE 19
Kathleen Turner (1954)
Phylicia Rashed (1948)
Pier Angeli (1932)
Gene Rowlands (1930)
Louis Jourdan (1919)
Mildred Natwick (1908)
Moe Howard (1897)
Charles Coburn (1877)
Dame Mae Whitty (1865)

## JUNE 20
Nicole Kidman (1967)
John Goodman (1952)
Stephen Frears (1941)
Martin Landau (1931)
Audie Murphy (1924)
Terence Young (1915)
Errol Flynn (1909)

# CANCER

## JUNE 21 — JULY 22

If someone had to give a thumbnail sketch of what it takes to make it in Hollywood, it would very likely sound a lot like a description of your typical Cancer. Those born under the sign of the Crab tend to be crusty, practical and hard-shelled on the outside, and sensitive, creative and emotional on the inside.

Cancers are the great nourishers of the zodiac, the maternal protectors of hearth and home. But as natural givers, they also crave emotional experience. And their tendency to cling to the past — be it social traditions or personal attachments to family and friends — bestows on them a mood-shifting temperament that translates easily into drama. In other words, Cancers can be touchy, but that's also what makes them so in touch with their feelings.

Cancers are so different on the outside from how they are on the inside that their "type" is difficult to pin down. You have to wonder how Tom Cruise, Tom Hanks and Yul Brynner were born under the same sign as Peter Lorre, David Spade and

Don Knotts. Or what Meryl Streep, Frances McDormand and Barbara Stanwyck have in common with Jane Russell, Pamela Lee and Courtney Love.

Some of the greatest directors ever to grace the screen are Cancers. But again, the range in style is confounding: Billy Wilder vs. Ingmar Bergman, William Wyler vs. Ken Russell, George Cukor vs. Mel Brooks.

The Cancer movie-lover is a sucker for movies about family and home, such as "Meet Me in St. Louis," "The Wizard of Oz" or "Cheaper by the Dozen." They're also domestic sensualists; in other words, they like to see the good life (even if it ends badly). Think "Titanic" or "The Stepford Wives." They also enjoy seeing good friends stick together, like in movies such as "The Big Chill," "Beaches" or "Return of the Secaucus Seven." What they definitely don't like are home-wreckers ("Fatal Attraction") or stories that threaten domestic stability ("Psycho" or "The Hand That Rocks the Cradle.")

Perhaps the ultimate Cancer is Jimmy Cagney. Renowned for his tough-guy gangster roles, he actually started out hoofing in vaudeville and often referred to himself as "just a dancer gone wrong." Talk about a deceptive outer shell. . . .

## FIVE SUGGESTED RENTALS

**"Cold Comfort Farm"** (1995)
Based on a popular 1932 book that deftly satirized the rustic rhapsodies of Hardy and Lawrence, John Schlesinger's sweet, savvy comic fable is one of the best things to hit a barnyard since "Babe." Think "Clueless" meets "Tobacco Road." Our heroine (Kate Beckinsale) is a sleek, sophisticated socialite whose parents have had the bad form to die without leaving her an inheritance. So she goes to live with her coun-

try cousins in Sussex and, with an "as if" aplomb worthy of Alicia Silverstone (or, actually, most Cancers), sets about tidying up the farm as well as her eccentric relatives' relatively cluttered lives. She's a matchmaker, a career counselor, an interior decorator, a Planned Parenthood advocate and even a gadget guru. Of course, in changing her kin, she changes herself from a self-involved know-it-all into a true Cancer caretaker. A witty, generous picture.

## "Kolya" (1997)

An Oscar-winner for best foreign language film, this beguiling Czech film takes place in Prague on the eve of the collapse of Communism. It's about a marriage of convenience (the groom gets money; the bride gets citizenship) that turns into an inconvenience when the new missus runs off, leaving her six-year-old son, Kolya (Andrej Chalimon) in the very reluctant hands of her abandoned "husband," Louka (Zdenek Sverak). A womanizing cellist who's barely scraping by, he's appalled. What's he supposed to do with a sniveling tot who doesn't even speak his language? The setup is familiar, but it's so well handled that it's irresistible. Cancers will be the most susceptible, but just about anyone will melt when this former cad and scoundrel bends down to tenderly tie the little boy's shoelace. Proving, I guess, that shamelessly affective mush really *is* a universal language.

## "Not Without My Daughter" (1991)

The made-for-TV title and the beginnnings of the Sally Field backlash made this a flop in the theaters, but it's one of the most gripping "motherhood is powerful" movies ever made. In 1984 (it's a true story), an American (Field) agreed to go with her young daughter and her Iranian husband (Alfred Molina) to visit his homeland. Once there, however, he insisted that they stay. For good. And while it's truly regrettable that parts of the film reinforce some of our ugliest sterotypes about Islamic culture, it's also true that Field's character became a virtual prisoner – relegated to to the subhuman status doled out to women by fundamentalist Moslems. The point of the movie isn't what's right or wrong with Iran; it could just as easily be about the once-sanctioned racism of South Africa. What matters most is its emotional power and its portrait of one woman's courage.

## "Unstrung Heroes" (1995)

A marvelous coming-of-age comedy/drama set in the early '60s. Twelve-year-old Stephen Lidz (Nathan Watt) has a young sister he likes to tease, a beautiful, loving mom (Andie MacDowell) he adores and a father who . . . well, let's just say dad (John Turturro), a self-styled inventor, is more nutty professor than parent, but he means well. All is well with the Lidz clan until the day Mom is diagnosed with cancer. Stephen escapes the aching reality of her illness by fleeing to the eccentric netherworld inhabited by his crackpot uncles (Maury Chaikin and Michael Richards). If Richards, Chaikin and Turturro are the film's splendid comic heart, MacDowell is its humane soul (Cancer's maternal essence at its best), giving a performance that refuses to be saccharine or saintly. The entire movie, in fact, is very Cancer-like – underneath its wacky shell is a tremendously tender and moving picture.

## "The Dead" (1987)

As purely perfect as the James Joyce short story on which it's based. Set in 1904 Dublin, the film focuses on an annual holiday party hosted by two elderly music teachers and its aftermath, in which the central character learns of a sad secret from his wife's past. The wife is played by Anjelica Huston, and this was her father John's last film. Not only is it an exquisite epitaph for a phenomenal career, but it's also a stunning convergence of two masters – Huston at eighty-one and Joyce at twenty-five. Interestingly, the older man's wisdom molds and mellows the younger man's severity – toward himself and his homeland. Joyce loved people more than he knew. But Huston knows, and that enriches the film. Cancers will embrace both the movie's domestic pleasures and its respectful remembrance of things past. And the final scene brings a sense of healing and peace as hushed as Joyce's famously falling snow.

## SIX TALENTED CANCERS

### Kathy Bates (June 28, 1948)

She won her Oscar for playing the crazed, ax-wielding fan in "Misery" who worships writer James Caan nearly to death. But Kathy Bates won our hearts for her work in films like "Fried Green Tomatoes," "Dolores Claiborne," "Primary Colors" and "Titanic" (as the unsinkable Molly Brown). Her talent is prodigious, but it's her naturalness that draws us to her. Though not a mother in real life, she projects a Cancer's maternal warmth and good common sense. Born in Memphis, Tennessee, she also has a Southerner's sense of history, which ties in nicely with Cancer's cling-to-the-past sensibility. Plus, she has Cancer's I-can-take-it outer shell. She's seen roles she created on stage go to Sissy Spacek and Michelle Pfeiffer on film ("'night Mother" and "Frankie and Johnny" respectively). She's not worried; too many people want to cast her in things she hasn't done before.

**Suggested Rental:** "Fried Green Tomatoes" (1991)
Here's a movie as cozy as your grandmother's antique quilt and every bit as artfully put together. Based on the best-seller by comic Fannie Flagg, the film offers parallel tales of friendship, love and liberation. In the present, elderly Jessica Tandy regales an overweight and underappreciated Bates with tales of the depression-era South. Her stories center around tiny Whistle Stop, Alabama, where tomboyish Mary Stuart Masterson and her best friend, Mary Louise Parker, run

the local café. On the surface, the material suggests terminal sitcom cutes, but director Jon Avnet and his top-notch cast transform it into something loving and lovely. Cancers will feel a natural kinship with this collection of nourishers of every possible stripe, as well as with its celebration of family in all its many forms. And like Bates, we become rapt listeners, waiting eagerly for Tandy to tell us what happened next.

**Cancer Moment:** Not only did Bates, in true Cancer style, thank her mother when she accepted her "Misery" Oscar, but she based a lot of her "Fried Green Tomatoes" performance on her Memphis upbringing. "I think a lot of my roots, teaching a child you had to behave in a certain way – you can't do that, you shouldn't do that, it's not done, what will people think – was part of the Southern heritage which I identified with in my character." She could've added that a lot of Cancers, Southern or not, are like that, too.

## Robin Williams (July 21, 1951)

The easiest way to characterize him is as our national class clown. But over the past two decades, Robin Williams has proven there's a lot more to him than "nanoo-nanoo" and speed-freak, stream-of-consciousness comic monologues. There's also intelligence, sweetness, thoughtfulness and sensitivity to other people. True, he can toss off imitations of everyone from Carol Channing to Pope John Paul II in a single interview. But that's part of his Cancer camouflage (and Crab-like, uncensored child-self). The funny stuff keeps us laughing, makes us feel taken care of (Cancer protectiveness). But it also keeps us from probing into the more complicated person underneath (Cancer self-protectiveness). He can do broad farce like "Mrs. Doubtfire," but it's roles in movies like his Oscar-winning "Good Will Hunting" – along with his work for Comic Relief – that reveal his true Cancer nature.

**Suggested Rental:** "Awakenings" (1990)
Just like most Cancers, this radiant movie is pure emotion — funny and depressing, wistful and uplifting. Set in 1969, it's based on the true story of a painfully shy doctor (Williams) who discovers a link among his catatonic patients: They all survived the sleeping sickness epidemic of the 1920s. When he tries a new drug on one of his living statues (Robert De Niro), a man who's been, for all intents and purposes, asleep for twenty years, the results are extraordinary in ways both good and bad. Working from Oliver Sacks's book, director Penny Marshall has made a life-affirming film about a human catastrophe and turned a failed miracle into a triumph. De Niro's is the showier role, but Williams provides the picture's subtle, caretaking heart. In a sense, it's a movie all about being a Cancer, as we watch these patients reveal the living human beings inside their initially unyielding outer shell.

**Cancer Moment:** In one of the film's most touching — and most difficult — scenes, the doctor's experimental treatment finally works and De Niro "awakens." According to Williams, his costar asked him to do something off-camera that would surprise him. "So I did Harvey Fierstein talking to him, 'Sweetheart, lose the puppy on the pajamas. Come over here, darling. Did Mom bring you that terrycloth robe? Do you want some slippers?'" If you're Robin Williams, you can turn something as sainted as maternal instinct into pure comic nonsense.

## Tom Cruise (July 3, 1962)

Being a heartthrob isn't as easy as it looks. But Tom Cruise makes it look easy. More important, he makes himself look for roles beyond the ones that only call for the megawatt grin and the perfect profile. Plus, he's sought out mentors like Paul Newman ("The Color of Money") and Dustin Hoffman ("Rain Man"). Part of the Brat

Pack generation of rising young studs, which included everyone from Rob Lowe to Emilio Estevez, he broke loose from the pack with "Risky Business" and never looked back. And while he's worked his gorgeous-guy charm in teeny-bop blockbusters like "Top Gun" and "Cocktail," he's also explored his darker side in films like "Interview with the Vampire" and "Jerry Maguire." He's the glam embodiment of Cancer's duality: Movie-star perfect on the outside (and able to use it) but moodier and more sensitive on the inside (and learning to use *that* as well).

**Suggested Rental:** "Rain Man" (1988)
Cruise didn't get an Oscar nomination for his performance in Barry Levinson's Academy Award winner, but he deserved one just as much as his costar, Dustin Hoffman (who won). In this fine film, Cruise is part of a reluctant brother act. He plays an L.A. sharpie who discovers that his father's will leaves everything to his brother (Hoffman), an autistic-savant who can memorize the phone book and do square roots in his head but thinks a candy bar costs $100. So he abducts his sibling from the institution where he's spent the last twenty years, and the pair embark on an odd-couple, cross-country odyssey. The movie's take-care-of-family theme is one Cancer will love. And it's especially moving to see how one brother finally breaks through his emotionally isolated shell and finds that genuine human contact can be a good thing. As you may have guessed, it's Cruise who makes the breakthrough.

**Cancer Moment:** During an interview, Cruise was asked what gave him the confidence to play in the big leagues with the likes of a Hoffman or a Newman. Like a true Cancer, he gave the credit to his mom, who kept the family together after a divorce. He said, "My mother said it didn't matter what you become, what's important is if you're happy and you enjoy it and you don't compromise yourself in any way."

## Meryl Streep (June 22, 1949)

Anything anyone else can do, Meryl Streep can probably do better, at least when it comes to acting. This prodigiously talented actress has put her Cancer sensitivity and adaptability to the test role after role. Accent jokes aside, she's convinced us she's a Danish writer/adventuress ("Out of Africa"); a Polish concentration camp survivor ("Sophie's Choice"); a blue-collar Australian mom ("A Cry in the Dark"); a Southern lobbyist ("The Seduction of Joe Tynan"); a frilly romance novelist ("She Devil"); a white-water champ ("The River Wild"); a neurotic, substance-abusing actress ("Postcards from the Edge"); a mysterious nineteenth-century tragic heroine ("The French Lieutenant's Woman"); and a transplanted Italian housewife stuck in the heartland ("The Bridges of Madison County"). She is a true Cancer caretaker in her work; we put ourselves in her hands and she does the rest.

**Suggested rental:** "Sophie's Choice" (1982)
It's Meryl's show. As William Styron's beautiful, tormented Polish-Catholic heroine — an enigmatic and guilt-ridden survivor of Auschwitz — Streep's performance elicits nothing but awe-struck superlatives. Her halting, intelligent delivery matches Sophie's mangled immigrant English effortlessly, and her character's mittel-European roots make perfect sense of Streep's broad brow and bumped nose. Yet she's never looked more beautiful; she gleams like white gold. The film is set in late '40s Brooklyn where a tragedy of love and death is played out by Sophie, her charismatic but unstable Jewish lover (Kevin Kline) and a struggling Southern writer (Peter MacNichol) who also is smitten with Sophie. The film lacks the weight of the novel, but Streep's portrayal is a marvel. And the titular choice will hit Cancers right where they live.

**Cancer Moment:** A maternal conundrum occurred during the filming. Streep had just had her first child, and when she came home at night after a day on the set, she still spoke in Sophie's guttural tones, which her baby didn't recognize and therefore would burst into tears. Her director, Alan J. Pakula, was both impressed and sympathetic to her devoted dual life. He told an interviewer, "Creative gifts, I think, are tougher for a woman than a man. To make all that work — playing Sophie, the emotional explosions, the terrors of that extraordinary role — and then to go home to her husband and son and make dinner!" Well, that's *precisely* what a Cancer would do.

## Harrison Ford (July 13, 1942)

We believe in Harrison Ford. We believe him when he's swashbuckling as Han Solo or Indiana Jones. We believe him as a kick-butt president ("Air Force One"); as a cynical gumshoe in a dessicated future ("Blade Runner"); as an amnesiac lawyer recovering from a trauma ("Regarding Henry"); and as a man wrongly accused of murder and on the run from a scene-stealing Tommy Lee Jones ("The Fugitive"). Well known for his little-known private life, he invariably adopts Cancer's protective shell in interviews. Journalists are always commenting on the outside wariness that, they assume, probably covers a brooding inner sensitivity (odds are, they're right). He was a carpenter before he became a star and he brings that same sense of craft to his career. And when the p.r. tours are done, he retreats, Crab-like, to his Wyoming home, to rejoin his wife, kids and real life.

**Suggested rental:** "Witness" (1985)
Ford received his only Oscar nomination for his role as a big-city cop assigned the case of a young Amish boy (Lukas

Haas) who, en route to visit relatives with his mother (Kelly McGillis), inadvertantly witnesses a murder in the Philadelphia train station. When Ford finds himself and his eyewitness at the center of a gathering storm of scandal and cover-ups, they flee back to the land of the hex sign and the horse-drawn carriage. Director Peter Weir turns the Pennsylvania Dutch countryside into a dreamscape, where wheat ripples like amber waves and a barn-raising seems sprung full-blown from an Aaron Copland symphony. The entire film is suffused with a Cancer's respect for family, the past and tradition. And when Ford and McGillis share a first – and last – dance to Sam Cooke's "What a Wonderful World It Would Be," all you can think is, what a wonderful movie it is.

**Cancer Moment**: One of the funniest bits in the film was a Ford ad-lib. His character is trying his best to adjust to the Amish regimen of getting up at 4:30 A.M. To him, it's still the middle of the night. Sitting down to breakfast, he breaks out into a broad, falsely hearty TV-commercial smile, raises his cup and says to McGillis, "Honey, that's a great cup of coffee." That's Cancer for you – home, hearth and humor.

## Barbara Stanwyck (July 16, 1907)

There wasn't one Barbara Stanwyck; there were dozens: among them, the shimmering seductress who tricks Fred MacMurray into doing her dirty work in "Double Indemnity;" the sharp-witted screwball heroine who has Henry Fonda literally falling all over himself in "The Lady Eve;" the wise-cracking reporter who wises up Gary Cooper in "Meet John Doe;" and the determined woman who kept William Holden in the ring (and in the film; Harry Cohn wanted him fired, but she fought to keep him) in "Golden Boy." She could be heroic ("Union Pacific") or hard-boiled

("Ball of Fire"), victim ("Sorry, Wrong Number") or victimizer ("The Strange Love of Martha Ivers"). Orphaned at age four, she followed her Cancer instincts by creating a "home" on her movie sets. To the world, she was Miss Barbara Stanwyck, but to the crews, who loved her for her nourishing unpretentiousness, she was always Missy.

**Suggested Rental:** "Stella Dallas" (1937)
This is the mother of all mother movies. It's about a coarse, blue-collar beauty (Stanwyck) who marries well, but alienates her society husband (John Boles) with her cheap, vulgar ways. They have a daughter, but soon divorce, and Stella raises the girl (Anne Shirley) on her own. When she realizes that her child is becoming increasingly embarrassed by her – visits with dad and his society friends don't help – she becomes the most self-sacrificing maternal figure this side of Bambi's mother ("Run for the thicket and don't look back!"). She purposely breaks with Shirley so the girl can leave her and go live guilt-free with her father. The movie is a Cancer-themed weep-a-thon, one of the purest, most unabashed celebrations of motherhood-as-martyrdom ever seen on screen. But it takes Stanwyck to make it work. Do not, under any circumstances, rent the 1990 Bette Midler version by mistake. Unless you hated your mother.

**Cancer Moment:** Producer Sam Goldwyn had to be convinced to cast Stanwyck. Not only did he think she was too young, but he felt she had never suffered for a child. She told him, "But I can imagine how it would be." Ironically, imagination was not her only tool. That very same year, disappointed and disinterested in her adopted son, Dion, she packed the six-year-old off to boarding school. The kid got her back years later by doing an interview with *Confidential* magazine called "Does My Mother, Barbara Stanwyck, Hate Me?"

# MOVIES "BORN" AS CANCERS

YOUNG MR. LINCOLN
BATMAN
DO THE RIGHT THING
WHEN HARRY MET SALLY
DAYS OF THUNDER
BOYZ N THE HOOD
REGARDING HENRY
A LEAGUE OF THEIR OWN
SLEEPLESS IN SEATTLE
THE FIRM

IN THE LINE OF FIRE
FREE WILLY
THE CLIENT
IL POSTINO (THE POSTMAN)
APOLLO 13
PHENOMENON
INDEPENDENCE DAY
COURAGE UNDER FIRE
MEN IN BLACK
CONTACT

## OTHER FAMOUS CANCERS

*Olympia Dukakis*

Bruce Campbell (1958)
Meryl Streep (1949)
Klaus Maria Brandauer (1944)
Michael Lerner (1941)
Kris Kristofferson (1936)
Ralph Waite (1929)
Billy Wilder (1906)

**JUNE 21**
Juliette Lewis (1973)
Michael Gross (1947)
Mariette Hartley (1940)
Joe Flaherty (1940)
Monte Markham (1935)
Olympia Dukakis (1931)
Maureen Stapleton (1925)
Judy Holliday (1922)
Jane Russell (1921)

**JUNE 23**
Frances McDormand (1957)
Bryan Brown (1947)
Bob Fosse (1927)
Irene Worth (1916)

**JUNE 24**
Nancy Allen (1950)
Peter Weller (1947)
Michele Lee (1942)
Chief Dan George (1899)

**JUNE 22**
Tracy Pollan (1960)

**JUNE 25**
Denys Arcand (1941)
June Lockhart (1925)
Sidney Lumet (1924)
Anne Revere (1903)
Charlotte Greenwood (1890)

**JUNE 26**
Chris O'Donnell (1970)
Josef Sommer (1934)
Eleanor Parker (1922)
Jay Silverheels (1919)
Peter Lorre (1904)

**JUNE 27**
Jason Patric (1966)
Isabelle Adjani (1955)
Krysztof Kieslowski (1941)

**JUNE 28**
Aileen Quinn (1971)
John Cusack (1944)
Mary Stuart Masterson (1966)
Alice Krige (1954)
Kathy Bates (1948)
Bruce Davison (1946)
Gilda Radner (1946)
Mel Brooks (1926)

**JUNE 29**
Amanda Donohoe (1962)
Gary Busey (1944)
Ian Bannen (1928)
Slim Pickens (1919)
Ruth Warwick (1916)
Bernard Hermann (1911)

Nelson Eddy (1901)

**JUNE 30**
Rupert Graves (1963)
Vincent D'Onofrio (1959)
Susan Hayward (1918)
Lena Horne (1917)
Anthony Mann (1906)

*Liv Tyler*

**JULY 1**
Liv Tyler (1977)
Pamela Anderson (1967)
Dan Aykroyd (1952)
Karen Black (1945)
Debbie Harry (1945)
Genevieve Bujold (1942)
Claude Berri (1934)
Sydney Pollack (1934)
Leslie Caron (1931)
Farley Granger (1925)
Constance Ford (1923)
Olivia De Havilland (1916)
William Wyler (1902)
Charles Laughton (1899)

**JULY 2**
Kathryn Erbe (1966)
Ron Silver (1946)
Kenneth McMillan (1932)

Brock Peters (1927)

**JULY 3**
Tom Cruise (1962)
Betty Buckley (1947)
Kurtwood Smith (1942)
Ken Russell (1927)
George Sanders (1906)

**JULY 4**
Victoria Abril (1957)
Stephen Boyd (1928)
Gina Lollabrigida (1927)
Neil Simon (1927)
Gloria Stuart (1910)
George Murphy (1902)
Louis Armstrong (1901)
Gertrude Lawrence (1898)
Louis B. Mayer (1882)

**JULY 5**
Shirley Knight (1937)
Katherine Helmond (1934)
Warren Oates (1928)
Jean Cocteau (1889)

*Sylvester Stallone*

**JULY 6**
Geoffrey Rush (1951)
Nathalie Baye (1948)

Sylvester Stallone (1946)
Ned Beatty (1937)
Della Reese (1931)
Donal Donnelly (1931)
Janet Leigh (1927)
Sebastian Cabot (1918)

**JULY 7**
Shelley Duvall (1949)
Ringo Starr (1940)
Vince Edwards (1928)
Vittorio De Sica (1901)
George Cukor (1899)

**JULY 8**
Kevin Bacon (1958)
Anjelica Huston (1951)
Kim Darby (1948)
Marty Feldman (1933)
Craig Stevens (1918)
Faye Emerson (1917)
Louis Jordan (1908)
Eugene Pallette (1889)

*Tom Hanks*

**JULY 9**
Fred Savage (1976)
Courtney Love (1965)
Kelly McGillis (1957)
Tom Hanks (1956)

Jimmy Smits (1955)
Chris Cooper (1951)
Brian Dennehy (1938)
Richard Roundtree (1937)

**JULY 10**
Arlo Guthrie (1947)
Sue Lyon (1946)
Nick Adams (1931)
Fred Gwynne (1926)
John Gilbert (1899)
Slim Summerville (1892)

**JULY 11**
Mark Lester (1958)
Sela Ward (1957)
Stephen Lang (1952)
Tab Hunter (1931)
Yul Brynner (1920)
Walter Wanger (1894)

**JULY 12**
Mel Harris (1956)
Cheryl Ladd (1951)
Bill Cosby (1937)
Jean Hersholt (1886)
Tod Browning (1882)

**JULY 13**
Cameron Crowe (1957)
Cheech Marin (1946)
Giancarlo Giannini (1942)
Harrison Ford (1942)
Robert Forster (1941)
Patrick Stewart (1940)

**JULY 14**
Jackie Earle Haley (1961)
Joel Silver (1952)
Polly Bergen (1930)
Nancy Olson (1928)
Harry Dean Stanton (1926)
Dale Robertson (1923)
Ingmar Bergman (1918)
Terry-Thomas (1911)
George Tobias (1901)
Donald Meek (1878)

**JULY 15**
Irene Jacob (1966)
Brigitte Nielsen (1963)
Forest Whitaker (1961)
Lolita Davidovich (1961)
Linda Ronstadt (1946)
Jan-Michael Vincent (1944)
Alex Karras (1935)
Nina Van Pallandt (1932)

**JULY 16**
Corey Feldman (1971)
Phoebe Cates (1963)
Ruben Blades (1948)
Corin Redgrave (1939)
Barnard Hughes (1915)
Sonny Tufts (1911)
Ginger Rogers (1911)
Barbara Stanwyck (1907)

**JULY 17**
Lucie Arnaz (1951)
Krzgsztof Zanussi (1939)
Diahann Carroll (1935)

Donald Sutherland (1934)
James Cagny (1899)

**JULY 18**
Elizabeth McGovern (1961)
James Brolin (1940)
Paul Verhoeven (1938)
Dolph Sweet (1920)
Red Skelton (1913)
Hume Cronyn (1911)
Lupe Velez (1908)
Chill Wills (1903)

**JULY 19**
Campbell Scott (1962)
Anthony Edwards (1962)
Atom Egoyan (1960)
George Dzundza (1945)
Richard Jordan (1938)
Pat Hingle (1924)
Lili Damita (1901)

**JULY 20**
Robert Rodriguez (1968)
Donna Dixon (1957)
Randal Kleiser (1946)
Diana Rigg (1938)
Natalie Wood (1938)

**JULY 21**
Lance Guest (1960)
Jon Lovitz (1957)
Robin Williams (1951)
Tony Scott (1944)
Edward Herrmann (1943)
Don Knotts (1924)

Ken Maynard (1895)

**JULY 22**
Charlotte Gainsbourg (1971)
David Spade (1965)
John Leguizamo (1965)
Joanna Going (1963)
Willem Dafoe (1955)
Albert Brooks (1947)
Danny Glover (1947)
Paul Schrader (1946)
Terence Stamp (1939)
Louise Fletcher (1934)
Orson Bean (1928)
Bryan Forbes (1926)
James Whale (1896)

# LEO

## JULY 23 — AUGUST 22

Wouldn't you know it? Leo the Lion is a Leo! The famous MGM trademark was "born" on July 31, 1928, when his roar was first heard at the New York premiere of "White Shadows in the South Seas."

The Cowardly Lion from "The Wizard of Oz" (Bert Lahr) is a Leo. So is "The Lion in Winter" (Peter O'Toole as Henry II). And, in a sense, so is "The Lion King," whose adult voice is provided by Leo Matthew Broderick. However, one famous Leo — Leonardo DiCaprio — is not. He's a Scorpio (November 11).

Those born under the sign of Leo traditionally love the spotlight, so it's no wonder that so many of them have been attracted to Hollywood careers. Charismatic extroverts, they can be leaders and they can be bullies. That probably explains why so many flamboyant, strong-minded directors were born Leos: Cecil B. DeMille, Alfred Hitchcock, John Huston, Sam Fuller, James Cameron, Roman Polanski, and Stanley Kubrick. However, the center of attention sometimes craves a larger audience than just the cast and crew on a movie set. Among the Leos who've roared to stardom are such famous names as Arnold Schwarzenegger, Wesley Snipes, Dustin Hoffman, Steve Martin, Whitney Houston, Sean Penn, Sandra Bullock, Madonna and Mae West. And it can't be just coincidence that so many flame-tressed beauties are fiery Leos: Maureen O'Hara, Arlene Dahl, Rhonda Fleming, Jill St. John, Sandra Bullock and Lucille Ball.

Leos love luxury, flamboyance and all the accouterments of the good life (including, apparently, a good tan; George Hamilton, who's approximately the color of Tandoori chicken, is a Leo). And, while they are the most egotistical of all the signs, they are also the most generous and big-hearted. Good movie choices for Leos would be films about powerful overachievers, driven to succeed at any cost, or films about royal succession, since thrones are very much to Leo's taste. Finally, anything with an opulent setting would appeal to Leo's extravagant nature. Leave the small, subtle films for someone else.

## FIVE SUGGESTED RENTALS FOR LEOS

### "Citizen Kane" (1941)

Perhaps the most celebrated power portrait Hollywood ever made. Wunderkind Orson Welles turned the town on its ear with his dazzling debut feature about the life and times of Charles Foster Kane (played, of course, by Welles). Yet the film is less a biography (though some insist Kane is a thinly disguised William Randolph Hearst) than a mystery. After Kane's death, a young reporter tries to solve the meaning behind his last gasp, "Rosebud." In seeking to unravel the conundrum of Kane's life — as publisher, industrialist and would-be politician — he finds many Kanes and a hall-of-mirror's worth of answers. Welles as Kane is probably one of the best examples of pure Leo ego ever captured on screen, and his power-mongering, big-spending ways are a natural attraction for Leo movie-lovers.

## "Evita" (1996)

Alan Parker's audacious adaptation of the Andrew Lloyd Weber/Tim Rice '70s pop opera gave rock goddess Madonna (another Leo) the chance to prove she could be a movie star after all. The picture, which plays like a music-video epic, brings together two Leo-like icons of blonde ambition: Madonna, a true master of modern celebrity self-promotion, and Eva Peron, who rose from small-town slut to the most powerful woman in Argentina in the late '40s and early '50s. The rich visuals and grandiose score are also up Leo's alley. And listen to this absolutely Leo lyric: "The people adore me/So Christian Dior me." In essence, she's the distaff version of Kane, buying priceless baubles instead of building grandiose estates, seducing a nation rather a series of unhappy wives.

## "The Lion King" (1994)

In true Leo style, this is the most successful of the neocycle of Disney animated classics which began with "The Little Mermaid" in 1989. Sort of "Hamlet" meets "Bambi" on the Serengeti, "The Lion King" follows the adventures of Simba, the lion cub (voiced first by Jonathan Taylor Thomas, then by Matthew Broderick), as he fights to regain the jungle throne that is rightfully his, after his evil uncle (Jeremy Irons arranges the death of Simba's father, the king (James Earl Jones). Add a touch of Borscht-veldt humor, courtesy of Nathan Lane and Ernie Sabella, and you've got royal entertainment for kids and kings. Leos will not only enjoy seeing their leonine alter ego so artfully animated, but they'll like the theme of enlightened monarchy. Which, of course, is how a Leo would run things.

## "The Age of Innocence" (1993)

Martin Scorsese deserted the mean streets of his beloved Little

Italy for this exquisite adaptation of Edith Wharton's prize-winning novel about New York society in the 1870s. Daniel Day-Lewis plays a socially prominent attorney torn between the well-bred debutante (Winona Ryder), to whom he's fashionably engaged, and her free-spirited cousin (Michelle Pfeiffer). Scorsese uses the opulence of the era — from the chandeliers to the china settings — to reflect the willful hypocrisy and dangerous liaisons of this gilded limbo. It's like watching a Mob hit at high tea. The setting, of course, has built-in Leo appeal, but so does the story, with its creme-de-la-creme intrigues among the upper crust. It's all about the "best" people who don't always do what's best for anyone else.

**"All About Eve"** (1950)
Fasten your seatbelts. As theatre diva Margot Channing, Bette Davis takes us on a tour-de-force ride through the back-biting and back-stabbing that are everday occurences backstage on Broadway. She gets excellent support from Anne Baxter as the scheming Eve of the title role and from George Sanders, Celeste Holm, Gary Merrill and Thelma Ritter as assorted theatrical folk (look for Marilyn Monroe in a small role). Until "Titanic" came along, this was the reigning movie as far as Oscar nominations, accruing a then-record 14. Even so, it took almost half a century for "Titanic" to tie it. Leos will be attracted to the film's actual Oscar gold (it won six, including best picture) and Davis's snarling, lioness-at-bay performance. When she roars, everybody listens.

## SIX TALENTED LEOS

**Lucille Ball** (August 6, 1911)
We learned to love Lucy on TV, but pretube, she had a long career that's a virtual history of the movies — Goldwyn Girl, bit player, supporting character ("Stage Door") and

finally, almost-star ("Fancy Pants" and "The Big Street"). Tough minded and ambitious, she was driven by Leo's blazing ego and imperious, I'll-try-that attitude to do things that women (at that time) usually didn't do. She married a younger man (Desi Arnaz), had her first child at thirty nine, and was president of the company she cofounded with Desi. Perhaps the stars wanted her on television. Certainly fate intervened when pregnancy forced her to drop out of "The Greatest Show on Earth" (she was replaced by Gloria Grahame). Being at loose ends, she started a sitcom — a little thing costarring Desi — called "I Love Lucy."

**Suggested Rental:** "Du Barry Was a Lady" (1943)
A huge hit on Broadway where it starred Ethel Merman and Bert Lahr, the movie was considerably refashioned as a vehicle for Red Skelton and Lucille Ball. Skelton plays a coatroom attendant with a huge, unrequited crush on a glamorous nightclub singer (Ball). After accidentally downing a loaded drink, he dreams he's Louis XV and Ball is the infamous courtesan-about-court, Madame Du Barry. Gene Kelly appears as Skelton's amorous rival, and Lana Turner has a walk-on as herself. And if you look closely at the bit players, you'll spot Ava Gardner and "Leave It To Beaver's" Hugh Beaumont. Though most critics compared it unfavorably to the show, Leos will like its dual dose of glamour: Versailles at the height of its gilded glory as imagined by MGM at the height of it's tinseled know-how.

**Leo Moment:** This is the movie that gave birth to Lucy's oh-so-Leo fiery red hair. The studio hair stylist, Sydney Guilaroff, decided to make her mousy hair roar. He declared, "The hair may be brown, but her soul is on fire." Lucy liked the look so much that she kept it for the rest of her life.

## Robert De Niro (August 17, 1943)

There's nothing in his looks to suggest a Leo, but De Niro's extraordinary on-screen charisma speaks louder than his coloring. And his best movie parts — in "Mean Streets," "Taxi Driver," "Raging Bull," "The King of Comedy," "The Godfather, Part II" and "GoodFellas" — burn with pure Leo ferocity. De Niro's celebrated total immersion in his roles is Leo ego turned inside out. No actor since Laurence Olivier has "hidden" himself so flamboyantly. Off-screen, he has a Leo's monarchlike presence and invincibility. Interviewers routinely call him distant and inscrutable, unfathomable and powerful. Yet his imperial reticence somehow never alienates reporters. The more regally unapproachable he is, the more they fawn. That's Leo power.

**Suggested Rental:** "Raging Bull" (1980)
A survey of leading critics named this Martin Scorsese film the best movie of the 1980s. Unfortunately, Oscar didn't feel the same way. The best picture prize that year went to "Ordinary People." However, De Niro won his second Oscar (his first was for "The Godfather, Part II") for his mesmerizing portrayal of boxer Jake La Motta, who comes off as part noble savage, part perversion of the American Dream. La Motta's life could be a cautionary tale for Leos: he went from King of the Ring and a self-made millionaire to an overweight, humiliated has-been. It's a classic case of "pride goeth before a fall," in or out of the boxing ring (La Motta admits that, once in a while, he took a dive at the behest of certain mobsters). But De Niro makes him a legendary figure, a corrupted brute force, punch-drunk brilliance gone to seed.

**Leo Moment:** In one of the most renowned obeisances to method acting ever made, De Niro gained sixty pounds to play the aging, washed-up former champ. De Niro's fight with fat

– "I reached the point where I couldn't tie my shoes," he told *Life* magazine – is a perverse triumph of Leo egomania; he will make himself repulsive because he so wills it.

## Alfred Hitchcock (August 13, 1899)

He said "Good eev-en-ing" like no one else, and he made movies the same way. The so-called "Master of Suspense" had a magical gift for cinematic story-telling, whether making subtle psychological thrillers like "Vertigo" and "Strangers on a Train," mainstream entertainment like "Rear Window" and "North by Northwest" or unabashed crowd-pleasers like "The Birds" and "To Catch a Thief." His Leo side emerges in his taste for golden-haired heroines, in his much-vaunted, ego-ridden need to control every aspect of his films and in his famous – though possibly apocryphal – declaration that "Actors should be treated like cattle." His Leo-like craving for recognition made him far more famous than most of the stars of his movies, and that was fine with him.

**Suggested Rental:** "Psycho" (1960)
Loosely based on the true story of Midwest mass murderer, Ed Gein, this film about the nasty doings at the Bates Motel has become part of our collective cinema memory. Once you've seen it, you can never, ever enter a shower at an unfamiliar roadside motel without the zing of Bernard Herrmann's frayed-nerve chords echoing in your head. However, amazingly, when the film was originally released, the critics were horrified. Bosley Crowther of the *New York Times* called it "a blot on an honorable career." Yet years later, Hitch's squalid saga of sicko mamma's boy, Anthony Perkins, and his unfortunate motel guest, Janet Leigh, would be declared a classic. The director took it in stride; he liked to say that his movies went from failures to masterpieces without ever being a success. Not true, but catchy.

**Leo Moment:** The famous shower scene is the director's equivalent of an actor's gaining sixty pounds to play a part (see De Niro, above). It exists as a tour-de-force showcase for Hitchcock's incredible manipulative skills and, as "Psycho" screenwriter, Joseph Stefano, has pointed out, this one sequence has generated more shot-by-shot analysis than any other in cinema history.

## John Huston (August 5, 1906)

In true Leo fashion, Huston was the center of attention in everything he did. For him, directing was as much an adventure as it was an art, thus his love for exotic film locales like Africa ("The African Queen") or Mexico ("The Night of the Iguana" and "The Treasure of the Sierra Madre"). Yet he could make any film into an adventure. The list of Huston-honed classics goes on and on: "The Maltese Falcon," "The Man Who Would Be King," "The Asphalt Jungle," "Wise Blood," "Prizzi's Honor" and "The Dead," to name just a few. Huston's inimitable Leonine presence was greatly enhanced by his distinctive voice. You may remember it best from "Chinatown," in which he plays Jack Nicholson's evil nemesis; it rumbles with Leo's authoritative thunder. He was a natural ruler, the man who could be king.

**Suggested Rental:** "The Man Who Would Be King" (1975) Huston had long wanted to film Rudyard Kipling's tale of the building of the Victorian Empire at its most grandiosely foolish. In fact, he worked on it for over three decades, beginning with Humphrey Bogart and Clark Gable. When that didn't happen, he tried again, this time with Paul Newman and Robert Redford in mind. Ultimately, he settled on Sean Connery and Michael Caine, which is another way of saying he "settled" for two of the best. They are perfect as a pair of grand rogues — sort of a split-personality version of the director – who try to take over a Himalayan kingdom with a bit of stiff-upper-lip British swagger and some smooth flim-flamming. A heroic, tragicomic meditation on the permutations of power, the movie has Leo confidence and noblesse-oblige generosity under difficult circumstances.

**Leo Moment:** The film was shot in Morocco, and Huston used some of the locals in small roles. According to his autobiography, "An Open Book," when he showed them the finished print, they told him, via an interpreter, "Now we will never die." A typical Leo yearning: to bestow immortality on others.

## Peter O'Toole (August 2, 1932)

From his feline grace to his leonine presence, O'Toole is everything a Leo should be – fair-skinned, golden-haired, with the roar of a legendary hell-raiser and the brilliance of someone regularly acknowledged as one of the greatest actors of his generation. Everything about him glistens with Leo's extravagance, from his acting to his reputation as an unparalleled pub-crawler (now retired). He shone magnificently in such diverse and unforgettable films as "Becket," "The Ruling Class," "The Stunt Man," "My Favorite Year" and "The Last Emperor." He's lent class to farces like "What's New Pussycat?" and disasters like "Caligula." To date, O'Toole has lost more Oscars (seven nominations, no wins) than any other actor. That probably says more about Oscar than it does about O'Toole.

**Suggested Rental:** "Lawrence of Arabia" (1962)
David Lean's desert classic won seven Oscars and made a then-unknown Irish actor named Peter O'Toole a star. It's the true story of T. E. Lawrence, the English eccentric and egoist, who united the feuding Arab tribes during World War 1 and led them to victory against England's enemy, the Turks. An

epic-scale adventure, it's also the story of a hugely conflicted man, torn between self-love and self-loathing (not an unfamiliar Leo dilemma, which they hide awfully well). Poised between a searing, clear-eyed intelligence and a soaring, blinders-on romanticism, the movie doesn't try to solve the enigma of Lawrence, who is a hero, a megalomaniac, and a deeply closeted homosexual. Rather, it presents him bathed in sunlight, his Bedouin robes billowing in the wind. He floats before us like the desert thing he is — more mirage than man.

**Leo Moment:** Even spectacularly beautiful people — many of whom are Leos — aren't beautiful enough for the movies. Before an inch of film was shot, O'Toole had to agree to a make-over — a nose job and a dye job that turned his hair the Leo-like blonde we know today. Hey, if it worked for Lucy . . .

## Robert Redford (August 18, 1937)

From his matinee-idol magnificence to his environmentally conscious generosity, Redford is the epitome of Leo-as-Golden Boy. He even has his own kingdom — the aptly named Sundance Institute where, every year, new princes of the American independent film are dubbed worthy of notice. Perhaps he isn't a Sun God in real life, but he could play one on TV (or in the movies). That's part of the Redford appeal, too; he refuses to exploit his supposed perfection. Instead, he's examined it in films like "The Candidate" and "The Way We Were." As adept at comedy/adventure ("Butch Cassidy and the Sundance Kid") as he is with "crusader" flicks ("All the President's Men"), he can't shake his Leo golden touch. The first time he tried directing ("Ordinary People"), he came home with an Oscar.

**Suggested Rental:** "The Electric Horseman" (1979)
Barely a blip on the screen compared to the other heavy-

weight titles in Redford's filmography, this is nonetheless a peerless bit of Hollywood entertainment – so slick that it doesn't seem slick. Redford plays a former rodeo champ feeling fenced in by his new role as a cereal shill. Jane Fonda costars as the intrepid girl reporter who joins him on his quixotic quest that ostensibly involves a horse (he's trying to save his mount from its corporate-decreed diet of steroids and pain-killers), but mostly involves matters of integrity. Considering when it came out, the movie sounds some early warning signals about ecology, consumerism and the image-is-all mentality of the advertising industry. Leos will like the way it skewers false arrogance and hollow glitz. They frankly prefer the real thing – in both cases.

**Leo Moment:** The idea for the film actually grew out of a previous picture, "Downhill Racer," which was loosely based on ski champ Jean-Claude Killy. In that film, Redford examined our obsession with winners (a very Leo theme). Then, some time later, he saw the once-great Killy reduced to capitalizing on his winner's reputation by pushing ski equipment. What struck him, Redford said, was "that switch, in a year, from shining victory to a vestige of that personality being exploited almost to death." The contrast was so striking that it became the germ for "The Electric Horseman." It's what a Leo would see best: magnificence ruined, majesty gone toxic.

## MOVIES "BORN" UNDER LEO

| | |
|---|---|
| MRS. MINIVER | UNFORGIVEN |
| THE FRESHMAN | RISING SUN |
| PRESUMED INNOCENT | THE FUGITIVE |
| HOT SHOTS | THE SECRET GARDEN |
| DOC HOLLYWOOD | THE MASK |
| DEATH BECOMES HER | WATERWORLD |
| BUFFY THE VAMPIRE SLAYER | BABE |

SOMETHING TO TALK ABOUT    TIN CUP
DANGEROUS MINDS    AIR FORCE ONE
THE USUAL SUSPECTS    PICTURE PERFECT

## OTHER FAMOUS LEOS

**JULY 23**
Marlon Wayans (1972)
Woody Harrelson (1961)
Ronny Cox (1938)
Jan Truell (1931)
Gloria DeHaven (1925)
Coral Browne (1913)
Harry Cohn (1891)

*Sandra Bullock*

**JULY 24**
Anna Paquin (1982)
Jennifer Lopez (1970)
Gus Van Sant (1952)
Michael Richards (1949)
Robert Hays (1947)
Chris Sarandon (1942)
Ruth Buzzi (1936)
Peter Yates (1929)

*Kevin Spacey*

Sandra Bullock (1965)
Kevin Spacey (1959)
Susan George (1950)
Helen Mirren (1946)
Mick Jagger (1943)
Peter Hyams (1943)

**JULY 25**
Brad Renfro (1982)
Matt LeBlanc (1967)
Illeana Douglas (1965)
Iman (1955)
Janet Margolin (1943)
Estelle Getty (1924)
Jack Gilford (1907)
Walter Brennan (1894)
Jeremy Piven (1965)

Stanley Kubrick (1928)
James Best (1926)
Jason Robards (1922)
Blake Edwards (1922)
Marjorie Lord (1918)
Vivian Vance (1913)
Gracie Allen (1902)

**JULY 27**
Jerry Van Dyke (1932)
Keenan Wynn (1916)
Charles Vidor (1900)
Donald Crisp (1880)

**JULY 28**
Elizabeth Berkley (1972)
Sally Struthers (1948)
Andrew V. McLaglen (1920)
Laird Cregar (1916)
Rudy Vallee (1901)
Joe E. Brown (1892)

**JULY 29**
Stephen Dorff (1973)
Ken Burns (1953)
Bill Forsyth (1946)
David Warner (1941)
Budd Boetticher (1916)
Thelma Todd (1905)
Clara Bow (1905)
William Cameron Menzies
  (1896)
William Powell (1892)
Theda Bara (1885)
Maria Ouspenskaya (1876)

**JULY 30**
Kerry Fox (1966)
Vivica A. Fox (1964)
Lisa Kudrow (1963)
Laurence Fishburne (1961)
Jean Reno (1948)
Arnold Schwarzenegger (1947)
Peter Bogdanovich (1939)

**JULY 31**
Wesley Snipes (1962)
Michael Biehn (1956)
Sherry Lansing (1944)
Geraldine Chaplin (1944)
Stanley R. Jaffe (1940)
France Nuyen (1939)
Don Murray (1929)

**AUGUST 1**
Dom Deluise (1933)
Geoffrey Holder (1930)
Arthur Hill (1922)

**AUGUST 2**
Edward Furlong (1977)
Kevin Smith (1970)
Mary-Louise Parker (1964)
Cynthia Stevenson (1963)
Joanna Cassidy (1944)
Max Wright (1943)
Wes Craven (1939)
Peter O'Toole (1932)
Carroll O'Connor (1925)
Beatrice Straight (1918)
Gary Merrill (1915)
Myrna Loy (1905)

**AUGUST 3**
John C. McGinley (1959)
John Landis (1950)
Martin Sheen (1940)
Gordon Scott (1927)
Marilyn Maxwell (1921)
Dolores Del Rio (1905)

## AUGUST 4
Billy Bob Thornton (1955)
Kristoffer Tabori (1952)
William Keighley (1889)

## AUGUST 5
Johnathan Silverman (1966)
Carole Laure (1951)
John Saxon (1935)
Zakes Mokae (1935)
Robert Taylor (1911)
John Huston (1906)
Reginald Owen (1887)

## AUGUST 6
Michelle Yeoh (1963)
Catherine Hicks (1951)
Dorian Harewood (1950)
Michael Anderson Jr. (1943)
Paul Bartel (1938)
Abby Lincoln (1936)
Andy Warhol (1928)
Frank Finlay (1926)
Ella Raines (1921)
Robert Mitchum (1917)
Lucille Ball (1911)
Hoot Gibson (1892)
Louella Parsons (1880)

## AUGUST 7
David Duchony (1960)
John Glover (1944)
Anjanette Comer (1943)
Verna Bloom (1939)
Nicholas Ray (1911)
Ann Harding (1901)

Billie Burke (1885)

*Dustin Hoffman*

## AUGUST 8
Martin Brest (1951)
Keith Carradine (1949)
Connie Stevens (1938)
Dustin Hoffman (1937)
Carl "Alfalfa" Switzer (1926)
Esther Williams (1923)
Rory Calhoun (1922)
Dino De Laurentis (1919)
Daniel Mann (1912)
Sylvia Sidney (1910)
Robert Siodmak (1900)

## AUGUST 9
Whitney Houston (1963)
Melanie Griffith (1957)
Sam Elliott (1944)
Leo Genn (1905)
Robert Aldrich (1918)
Robert Shaw (1927)
Charles Farrell (1901)

## AUGUST 10
Rosanna Arquette (1959)
Eddie Fisher (1928)
Martha Hyer (1924)
Rhonda Fleming (1923)

# LEO

Jeff Corey (1914)
Mae Clarke (1910)
Norma Shearer (1900)
Jack Haley (1899)
Walter Lang (1896)

## AUGUST 11
Hulk Hogan (1953)
Ian Charleson (1949)
Anna Massey (1937)
Arlene Dahl (1924)
Lloyd Nolan (1902)

## AUGUST 12
George Hamilton (1939)
John Derek (1926)
Sam Fuller (1912)
Cantinflas (1911)
Jane Wyatt (1911)
Oscar Homolka (1898)
Cecil B. DeMille (1881)

## AUGUST 13
Neville Brand (1921)
Gene Raymond (1908)
Regis Toomey (1902)
Alfred Hitchcock (1899)
Bert Lahr (1895)

*Steve Martin*

## AUGUST 14
Romaine Bohringer (1973)
Halle Berry (1968)
Emmanuelle Beart (1965)
Susan Saint James (1946)
Wim Wenders (1945)
Steve Martin (1945)
Lina Wertmuller (1928)
Alice Ghostly (1926)
Nehemiah Persoff (1920)

## AUGUST 15
Natasha Henstridge (1974)
Ben Affleck (1972)
Debi Mazar (1964)
Tess Harper (1950)
Abby Dalton (1935)
Janice Rule (1931)
Nicholas Ray (1928)
Huntz Hall (1919)
Wendy Hiller (1912)
Ethel Barrymore (1879)

## AUGUST 16
Timothy Hutton (1960)
Angela Bassett (1958)
Madonna (1958)
James Cameron (1954)
Lesley Ann Warren (1946)
Bob Balaban (1945)
Bruce Beresford (1940)
Lorraine Gary (1939)
Anita Gillette (1936)
Julie Newmar (1935)
Robert Culp (1930)
Ann Blyth (1928)

Fess Parker (1925)
Glenn Strange (1899)

**AUGUST 17**
Sean Penn (1960)
Robert Joy (1951)
Robert De Niro (1943)
Maureen O'Hara (1920)
Mae West (1893)
Monty Woolley (1888)

**AUGUST 18**
Christian Slater (1969)
Madeleine Stowe (1958)
Denis Leary (1957)
Patrick Swayze (1952)
Martin Mull (1943)
Robert Redford (1937)
Roman Polanski (1933)
Shelley Winters (1922)
Alain Robbe-Grillet (1922)
Marcel Carne (1909)

**AUGUST 19**
Matthew Perry (1969)
Kyra Sedgwick (1965)
Kevin Dillon (1965)
Peter Gallagher (1956)
Jonathan Frakes(1952)
Dawn Steel (1946)
Jill St. John (1940)
Debra Paget (1933)
Gene Roddenberry (1921)
Marie Wilson (1916)
Claude Dauphin (1903)

**AUGUST 20**
Joan Allen (1946)
Peter Horton (1953)
Isaac Hayes (1942)
Fay Holder (1895)

**AUGUST 21**
Kim Cattrall (1956)
Peter Weir (1944)
Melvin Van Peebles (1932)
Barry Foster (1931)
Maurice Pialat (1925)
Jack Weston (1924)

**AUGUST 22**
Cindy Williams (1947)
Diana Sands (1934)
Honer Blackman (1926)
Leni Riefenstahl (1902)
Elizabeth Bergner (1897)

# VIRGO

## AUGUST 23 — SEPTEMBER 22

A Hollywood virgin would seem to be an oxymoron. Yet a surprising number of Virgos — that is, those born under the sign of the Virgin — have made it big in the movies.

One explanation is that Virgos are notoriously industrious and methodical, talents that serve them well when negotiating the labyrynthian power structure (and equally labyrynthian egos) of the film business.

Another explanation is that Virgos aren't necessarily "virginal." Rather, they are intelligent and discriminating, with a natural bent toward perfectionism. Hence the proliferation of Virgo directors, ranging from Preston Sturges and Jean Renoir to Tim Burton and Oliver Stone.

They are also a sign celebrated for their physical beauty. Leading ladies born under Virgo include Greta Garbo, Ingrid Bergman, Claudette Colbert, Lauren Bacall, Sophia Loren and Jacqueline Bisset. More recent names are Rebecca De Mornay,

Cameron Diaz and Salma Hayek.

Men include such classic profiles as Fredric March, Sean Connery, Richard Gere, Jean-Louis Barrault, and Alan Ladd. On the younger side, try lookers like Keanu Reeves, Hugh Grant, Charlie Sheen and Blair Underwood.

The Virgo gift for detail makes them a natural for comedy, where precison and meticulous preparation are usually behind the most "spontaneous" gag. Some famous funny folk born Virgos are Peter Sellers, Lily Tomlin, Bill Murray, Jason Alexander, Michael Keaton, Joan Blondell, Damon Wayans and Paul Reubens.

The Virgo movie-goer is a sort of amateur film critic, bringing with him or her a keen sense of whether or not picture is working. They like their movies to be well made and to make sense. The "Police Academy" series or anything with the word "Porky's" in it are not good bets for Virgos.

## FIVE SUGGESTED MOVIES FOR VIRGOS

**"The Remains of the Day"** (1993)
Virgo is a serious sign of service, and few movies have captured the essence of the serving class as it was in the days of England's more stately mansions as well as this James Merchant-Ismail Ivory film, which stars Anthony Hopkins and Emma Thompson. An adaptation of Kazuo Ishiguro's acclaimed book, the picture is also a deft study of another Virgo trait: repression. Hopkins is the head of the household, and Thompson is a member of his staff. Together they create a beautifully-acted meditation of the road not taken, or, rather, the life not lived. The movie also can be viewed as a cautionary tale, a warning against taking one's Virgo bent for self-denial and sense of duty too far.

## "Star Trek: The Wrath of Khan" (1982)

No telling if they have horoscopes on the planet Vulcan, but if so, Mr. Spock (Leonard Nimoy) would have to have been born a Virgo. Think about it: analytical, logical, precise, excellent at supressing his emotions. The second in this hugely successful series, this picture is easily the best of the lot. Director Nicholas Meyer gives the film pace, humor and excitement while working all sorts of variations on beloved "Star Trek" formulas. William Shatner and villain Ricardo Montalban try to out-ham each other, while Nimoy gets to make the logical sacrifice for the greater good. One touch that will appeal to duty-bound Virgos: the movie's assumption that right and wrong exist, even in zero gravity.

## "The English Patient" (1996)

For all their surface fussiness, Virgos are also incurable romantics. This Oscar-winner is an incurably romantic movie, built around Virgo-approved motifs of sacrifice, propriety and duty. Director Anthony Minghella mixes the old-fashioned grandeur of a David Lean film with a fragmented narrative geared to the synapses of an MTV audience. Near the end of World War II, a hideously scarred Englishman (Ralph Fiennes) is tended to by a nurse (Oscar winner Juliet Binoche) with scars of her own. Meanwhile, opium-induced oases of Fiennes' memory take us back to pre-war North Africa where he was a dashing map-maker having an affair with a married aristocrat (Kristen Scott-Thomas).

## "The Dresser" (1983)

The life of service takes center-stage in this terrific film starring Albert Finney and Tom Courtenay (both Oscar nominees). Here, all the world's a stage — especially backstage, where Sir (Finney), a grandiose but aging star, and Norman (Courtenay), his devoted dresser, play Lear and his Fool, who are both stranded on the howling heath that is a life in the theater. The year is 1940 and as German planes buzz over-

head, Norman struggles to get Sir through his 227th performance of "King Lear." Finney plays a magnificent ruin magnificently — a blend of sham, ham and genius. But Virgos will
more likely be drawn to Norman, a flitting factotem whose
entire life is bound up in his relationship to Sir.

**"The Draughtsman's Contract"** (1982) Peter Greenaway's film
is like a Restoration play written by cartoonist Edward Gorey.
Insidiously wicked and visually dazzling, the movie takes place
in gilded seventeenth-century England, where the only thing
more overcultivated than the manners and the clothing are the
gardens. An arrogant architect (Anthony Higgins) signs an
unusual contract with a noblewoman (Janet Suzman). He's to
create twelve drawings of her husband's magnificent estate; in
return, she must grant him the same number of sexual favors.
Mocking in its chilly elusiveness, seductive in its suggestive alle-
gories, the entire picture is a tantalizing puzzle that should
delight the analytical, discriminating and oh-so-clever Virgo.

## SIX TALENTED VIRGOS

**Oliver Stone** (September 15, 1946)
The hot-headed, self-described "cinematic
provocateur" isn't exactly the image of the
cool, self-effacing Virgo. But Stone's Virgo
side surfaces in his obsessive attention to
detail and his voracious appetite for analysis
and truth-seeking, as evidenced in "Platoon"

and "JFK." Plus, like a true Virgo, Stone often throws himself
into movie-making with a greater good in mind, whether it's
a defense of the anti-war '60s ("Born on the Fourth of July")
or a condemnation of the '80s "greed is good" mentality
("Wall Street"). His often bombastic style may seem the
opposite Virgo's ingrained, don't-mind-me sense of propriety.
But deep down, he's a very Virgo pure-of-heart social critic.

**Suggested Rental:** "Nixon" (1995)

Stone's intricate, compassionate, highly ambitious character study of the only man ever forced to resign the presidency follows Richard M. Nixon (Anthony Hopkins) from his dirt-poor childhood to his dirty-politics downfall; that is, Boy meets Oval Office, Boy gets Oval Office, Boy loses Oval Office, End of Story. Stone treats Nixon much like a Shakespearian king — not a tragic Lear, but more like a Richard II. That is, a man of power brought low by a fateful combination of circumstance and his own character flaws. It is, in a sense, the saddest story you'll ever see, about a man who worked extra hard (Virgo!) and got everything he wanted. And then it got him back.

**Virgo Moment:** Hopkins's repressed yet sympathetic portrayal shows us a man who knew both too much and too little about himself (something that applies to Virgos, who often are mired in details). In one unforgettable scene, Nixon/Hopkins stands by a portrait of his nemesis, John Kennedy, and says, "When they look at you, they see what they want to be. When they look at me, they see what they are." This illustrates Virgo perspicacity in a nutshell, searingly self-critical yet undeniably accurate.

**Tommy Lee Jones** (September 15, 1946) As the obsessed, humorless alien-hunter in "Men in Black," Jones takes the Virgo stereotype (dry, methodical, exacting, dedicated) to a hilarious extreme. Though he's proven himself capable of handling leading-man parts ("Lonesome Dove"), Jones truly shines in off-beat roles, such as Sissy Spacek's loving but abusive husband in "Coal Miner's Daughter"; the colorful and elusive Clay Shaw in "JFK"; and an antiheroic Ty Cobb in "Cobb." His Virgo side emerges in his exacting forcefulness; you don't mess around with Tommy Lee. And, like all true Virgos, he simply gets the job done, with cool professionalism and an eye fixed unwaveringly on his goal.

**Suggested Rental:** "The Fugitive" (1993)
This crackerjack, fast-on-its-feet thriller owes less to David Janssen's long-running TV series than it does to Hitchcock's "wrong man" movies. Harrison Ford has the Janssen role — a prominent surgeon falsely convicted of killing his wife and on the run from a relentless Javert-like U.S. marshal (Jones). The film is a nonstop chase that makes a virtual art out of the close call, as Ford keeps narrowly escaping from the tenacious Tommy Lee. Ford gets to glower handsomely and do his wonderful "what-me-worry?" haunted bit. But Jones gets the good lines. He got the Oscar, too, for best supporting actor. Virgos will have to restrain themselves from cleaning up the mess after the movie's famous train crash.

**Virgo Moment:** Giving a human dimension to a hardened professional, Jones's dry wisecracks to his subordinates are the essence of Virgo's pithy sense of humor. In the film's most famous exchange, Ford, holding a gun on Jones, protests his innocence, to which Jones bluntly replies, "I don't care." Jones later told an interviewer he felt that line was the key to the character: "Here's a guy who says quite truthfully to a man with a gun, 'I don't care if you killed your wife or not. You're gonna get caught. Kill me. You're gonna get caught.'" Spoken like a true Virgo.

## Hugh Grant (September 9, 1960)

On screen and in interviews, this handsome British actor plays the bashfully self-effacing Virgo archetype to perfection. A certain "Divine" night in L.A. aside, Grant seems to be his characters — bright, endearingly awkward, waggishly self-deprecating. While comparisons to another Grant named Cary may be presumptive, this Grant offers much the same package: oodles of charm wrapped in great looks and an ingratiating accent. As for his becoming typecast as the sexually repressed British gentleman ("Sirens," "Impromptu" and "Sense and Sensibility"), he's defended his choices in interviews, saying, "They're not exactly repressed. They're just English." A nice touch of Virgo's sly wit.

**Suggested Rental:** "Four Weddings and a Funeral" (1994)
As sweetly funny as a rehearsal-dinner toast among old friends and as disposable as a bridesmaid's dress, this comedy not only made Grant a star, but solidified his image as the fastidous, adorably befuddled, eternally boyish Brit. He plays a winsome bachelor — the always-the-groomsman-never-the-groom type — who meets an equally charming American (Andie MacDowell) at a mutual friend's nuptials. His not-quite-pursuit of her is the main plot, but the bulk of the film is concerned with the delicate balance of emotion and humor inherent to time-honored rituals. This dapper valentine of a picture delivers even more than it promises: four weddings, a funeral and a happy ending.

**Virgo moment:** After the movie became a worldwide hit, Grant won a Golden Globe Award for Best Actor. His acceptance speech was a high point of the evening. "It's tragic how much I'm enjoying this," he said, statue in hand. "It's with tremendous ill grace that I grudgingly acknowledge the contributions of a few other people." He then went on to thank everyone from his director, Mike Newell, to his girlfiend, Elizabeth Hurley. It was a perfect Virgo artifice — dry, clever, well-constructed, crisply amusing and very, very effective.

**Jeremy Irons** (September 19, 1948)
In Jeremy Irons, Virgo's trademark fastidious-
ness becomes ever-so-elegant, but also a little malevolent and a little warped. Witness
his superb work as deranged twin doctors in
"Dead Ringers" or his oh-so-respectable
British politician who has a torrid affair with his son's fiancee
in "Damage." But whether he's playing heroes ("The French
Lieutenant's Woman") or adulterers ("Betrayal"), Irons projects a Virgo's discriminating intelligence and somehow sexy
aloofness. Early in his career, he expressed admiration for his
character in "Brideshead Revisited," saying, "I think discipline
and difficulty do increase pleasure when it's finally attained.
But that's because I'm a puritan." And a Virgo.

**Suggested Rental:** "Reversal Of Fortune" (1990)
Irons won a well-deserved Oscar for this enticing tragicomedy of bad manners. Director Barbet Schroeder (another Virgo)
delivers a "Lifestyles of the Rich and Infamous," based on the
real-life case of Claus von Bulow, who was charged with trying to kill his wealthy wife, socialite Sunny von Bulow (Glenn
Close), with an insulin overdose. The movie focuses on the
odd coupling of von Bulow (Irons), the chilly, snobbish
European, and his lawyer, Alan Dershowitz (Ron Silver), the
quintessential, go-getting ethnic American. There's too much
Dershowitz and too little dirt, but it doesn't matter, since the
film lives and breathes Irons's performance — a masterwork
of audacious ambiguity and arrogant insinuation.

**Virgo Moment:** With typical Virgo thoroughness, Irons
researched his role by pouring over old TV interviews with von
Bulow and videotapes of the trial. While making the movie,
however, he let his Virgo self-critical side get out of hand.
Schroeder remembers that after one scene, Irons approached
him and protested that he hadn't given him enough notes on
what he was doing wrong. Schroeder replied, "Why should I?

You leave me speechless." A telling exchange of Virgo perfectionism from both men.

## Lauren Bacall (September 16, 1924)

There are two Lauren Bacalls: the sultry '40s ingenue who seduced the world in general – and Humphrey Bogart in particular – with her insinuating style and drop-dead looks, and the still-sexy, self-confident veteran with the smoky voice and the grand-dame demeanor. The former has Virgo's hard-work ethic. The latter reveals Virgo's demanding, critical nature. It was rumored that Bacall lost her best supporting actress Oscar bid for "The Mirror Has Two Faces" because, in real life, she's much like her character: emphatic, blunt, difficult. But Oscar winner or not, she is Virgo as eternal legend, with nothing to prove anymore to anyone. Formidable, yes, but deservedly so.

**Suggested Rental:** "The Big Sleep" (1946)
A whodunit's whodunit, this brash film noir is outrageous fun with a twist. Quite simply, nobody involved with the picture, including Raymond Chandler who wrote the book, was ever quite sure whodunit or why. Bogart is cynicism in a trenchcoat as private eye Philip Marlowe, hired to sort out – and hush up – some compromising matters involving a decadent millionaire and his two daughters. Bacall plays the older sister as a welcome antidote to every dumb Hollywood blonde there ever was; she's languid, sensuous and utterly dangerous. Ultimately, whodunit doesn't matter. When Bogart and Bacall are together, trading loaded double entendres and even more loaded glances, the screen sizzles.

**Virgo Moment:** In her second autobiography, "Me," Bacall says she got the acting lesson of her life while making "The Big Sleep." In one scene, Bogart gave her some advice before the cameras rolled, telling her, "You don't just walk to the door because the director says, 'Action.'" Bacall muses in her book, "That's what acting is, really. No breast-beating, no big motivation discussion. Just thought, focus, logical thinking." In other words, the Virgo approach to just about anything.

## Ingrid Bergman (August 29, 1915)

In movies, she radiated a virginal saintliness that made her perfect for roles as a nun ("The Bells of St. Mary's"), a martyr ("Joan of Arc") and, of course, the most famous inspiration for noble sacrifice in all of cinema: "Casablanca." But off screen, she was a complex, ambitious and passionate woman who got herself in some very un-Virgo-like hot water when she left her family to run off with Roberto Rossellini. Still, she's at her most Virgo in her devotion to her art. Nothing mattered to her more than acting — not her husband, her daughter, her reputation or, ultimately, Rossellini. She's the essence of Virgo's discipline filtered through an enormous talent.

**Suggested Rental:** "Autumn Sonata (1978)
In her last feature role, Bergman takes on an audaciously self-revealing challenge as a celebrated concert pianist who sacrificed her family and her personal life for her career (sound anything like Bergman's real life?). Directed by that other famous Bergman, Ingmar, the movie begins when she's reunited with her neglected grown-up daughter (Liv Ullmann) after seven years. The pair embark on a painful long day's journey into night as the embittered Ullmann lets loose her furious recriminations on her willful, self-centered parent. Bergman (Ingrid, not Ingmar), who'd already won three Oscars, received yet another nomination for her performance in this film.

**Virgo Moment:** The perfectionism and all-consuming dedication to her art evinced by Bergman's character will be familiar to Virgos. So will her discriminating, critical nature, which surfaces most clearly in an excruciatingly well-observed scene in which Ullmann plays a Chopin prelude for her mother. Mom, in turn, can't help sitting down and performing the same piece with the expertise and shadings of a true artist. Ullmann, of course, is humiliated, while Bergman, of course, is oblivious to the hurt she's inflicted. She's simply done the job as it should be done.

## FAMOUS MOVIES "BORN" UNDER VIRGO

| | |
|---|---|
| BARTON FINK | SLACKERS |
| THE FIRST WIVES CLUB | ONE FALSE MOVE |
| THE GAME | BOB ROBERTS |
| GOODFELLAS | SCHOOL TIES |
| MARY POPPINS | INTO THE WEST |
| POSTCARDS FROM THE EDGE | THE AGE OF INNOCENCE |
| QUIZ SHOW | NATURAL BORN KILLERS |
| SEA OF LOVE | BLUE SKY |
| SHIRLEY VALENTINE | FLY AWAY HOME |
| SNEAKERS | THE WITCHES |

## OTHER TALENTED VIRGOS

**AUGUST 25**
Tim Burton (1958)
Tom Skerritt (1943)
Sean Connery (1930)
Van Johnson (1916)
John Badham (1939)
Anne Archer (1947)

**AUGUST 26**
Macaulay Culkin (1980)
Barbet Schroeder (1941)

**AUGUST 27**
Paul Reubens (1952)
Barbara Bach (1947)
Tuesday Weld (1943)

## AUGUST 28
Daniel Stern (1957)
Pat Morita (1932)
Ben Gazzara (1930)
Donald O'Connor (1925)
James Wong Howe (1899)
Charles Boyer (1899)

## AUGUST 29
Rebecca De Mornay (1961)
Michael Jackson (1958)
Joel Schumacher (1939)
William Friedkin (1939)
Elliott Gould (1938)
Sir Richard Attenborough
  (1923)
Preston Sturges (1898)

*Cameron Diaz*

## AUGUST 30
Cameron Diaz (1972)
David Paymer (1954)
Timothy Bottoms (1951)
John Landis (1950)
Elizabeth Ashley (1939)
Fred MacMurray (1908)
Shirley Booth (1907)
Joan Blondell (1906)
Raymond Massey (1896)

*Richard Gere*

## AUGUST 31
Richard Gere (1939)
James Coburn (1928)
Richard Basehart (1914)
Buddy Hackett (1924)
Dore Schary (1905)
Fredric March (1897)

## SEPTEMBER 1
Lily Tomlin (1939)
Ron O'Neal (1937)
Richard Farnsworth (1920)
Vittorio Gassman (1922)
Yvonne De Carlo (1922)
Richard Arlen (1899)

## SEPTEMBER 2
Salma Hayek (1966)
Keanu Reeves (1964)
Mark Harmon (1951)

## SEPTEMBER 3
Charlie Sheen (1965)
Pauline Collins (1940)
Eileen Brennan (1935)
Anne Jackson (1925)
Alan Ladd (1913)

## SEPTEMBER 4
Ione Skye (1970)
Damon Wayans (1960)
Judith Ivey (1951)
Richard Castellano (1933)
Jan Swankmayer (1934)
Leonard Frey (1938)
Mitzi Gaynor (1930)

*Michael Keaton*

## SEPTEMBER 5
Michael Keaton (1951)
Werner Herzog (1942)
Raquel Welch (1940)
Joan Sydney (1938)
Jack Buetel (1915)
William Devane (1937)
Darryl F. Zanuck (1902)

## SEPTEMBER 6
Rosie Perez (1964)
Jane Curtin (1947)
Swoosie Kurtz (1944)

## SEPTEMBER 7
Julie Kavner (1951)
Peter Lawford(1923)
Anthony Quayle (1913)
Elia Kazan (1909)

## SEPTEMBER 8
David Arquette (1972)
Jonathan Taylor Thomas (1981)
Virna Lisi (1937)
Peter Sellers (1925)
Sid Caesar (1922)
Jean-Louis Barrault (1910)

## SEPTEMBER 9
Henry Thomas (1971)
Adam Sandler (1966)
Sylvia Miles (1932)
Topol (1935)
George Lazenby (1939)
Cliff Robertson (1924)
Max Reinhardt (1873)
Arthur Freed (1894)

## SEPTEMBER 10
Colin Firth (1960)
Chris Columbus (1958)
Amy Irving (1953)
Judy Geeson (1948)
Robert Wise (1914)
Edmond O'Brien (1915)

## SEPTEMBER 11
Harry Conick Jr. (1967)
Virginia Madsen (1963)
Kristy McNichol (1962)
Amy Madiagn (1950)
Earl Holliman (1928)
Brian De Palma (1940)

**SEPTEMBER 12**
Rachel Ward (1957)
Jacqueline Bisset (1944)
Ian Holm (1931)
Freddie Jones (1927)
Ben Blue (1901)
Claudette Colbert (1903)
Maurice Chevalier (1888)

**SEPTEMBER 13**
Richard Kiel (1939)
Scott Brady (1924)
Maurice Jarre (1924)
Jesse L. Lasky (1880)

**SEPTEMBER 14**
Kimberly Williams (1971)
Nicol Williamson (1938)
Sam Neill (1947)
Harve Presnell (1933)
Clayton Moore (1914)
Alain Cavalier (1931)
Jack Hawkins (1910)
Hal B. Wallis (1899)

**SEPTEMBER 15**
Jackie Cooper (1921)
Margaret Lockwood (1911)
Fay Wray (1907)
Jean Renoir (1894)

**SEPTEMBER 16**
Jennifer Tilly (1961)
Mickey Rourke (1956)
Anne Francis (1932)
Peter Falk (1927)

Alexander Korda (1893)
George Chakiris (1933)
Ed Begley Jr. (1949)

**SEPTEMBER 17**
Rita Rudner (1955)
John Ritter (1948)
Roddy McDowall (1928)
Anne Bancroft (1931)
Edgar G. Ulmer (1904)
Ben Turpin (1874)

*Jada Pinkett*

**SEPTEMBER 18**
Jada Pinkett (1971)
Fred Willard (1939)
Jack Warden (1920)
Greta Garbo (1905)
Jack Cardiff (1914)
Eddie "Rochester" Anderson
   (1905)
Robert Blake (1933)
Rossano Brazzi (1916)
Frankie Avalon (1939)

**SEPTEMBER 19**
Kevin Hooks (1958)
David McCallum (1933)
Rosemary Harris (1930)
Frances Farmer (1914)

Porter Hall (1888)

**SEPTEMBER 20**
Anne Meara (1929)
Sophia Loren (1934)
Rachel Roberts (1927)
Fernando Rey (1917)
Kenneth More (1914)

**SEPTEMBER 21**
Ricki Lake (1968)
Ethan Coen (1957)
Bill Murray (1950)
Nick Castle (1947)
Caleb Deschanel (1941)
Henry Gibson (1935)
Gail Russell (1924)
Chuck Jones (1911)

**SEPTEMBER 22**
Paul LeMat (1946)
Martha Scott (1914)
John Houseman (1902)
Erich Von Stroheim (1885)

# LIBRA

## SEPTEMBER 23 — OCTOBER 22

Libras are lovely — lovely to look at and lovely to be with. In fact, you'd think Hollywood would be the last place to attract a sign so devoted to harmony and balance. But you'd be wrong.

Libras are enormously creative. Plus, their taste for lovely things can easily translate into an attraction for the manufactured perfection of motion pictures. They're also gifted diplomats. They go along to get along, with a built-in head-in-the sand quality that buries the past and concentrates on the present. Certainly handy when last week's enemy is this week's costar.

And then there's the physical thing. All that proportion, fairness and charm poured into a perfect profile or a gorgeous body (say, Catherine Deneuve, Brigitte Bardot, Rita Hayworth, Neve Campbell and Gwyneth Paltrow). Equally Libran are such well-balanced leading ladies as Julie Andrews, Greer Garson, Lillian Gish, Deborah Kerr and Sigourney Weaver. As for typical Libra males, try Montgomery Clift, Christopher

Reeve, Marcello Mastroianni, Michael Douglas, Armand Assante and Sting.

Libras don't like people to dislike them, and they can be infuriatingly indecisive, so directing isn't necessarily their first choice. Yet, they're such great diplomats and natural aesthetes that they've had success behind the camera, too: Penny Marshall, Arthur Penn, Michael Powell, David Zucker, John Sayles, and Jim Henson.

The Libra movie-goer loves lovely looking movies. And lovely sounding ones — music is a big factor for Libras. And remember, Libra's sign is the Scales. Movies that favor extremism over equality, bizarreness over grace are not their style (say, anything by Oliver Stone or John Waters.) And, while Ed Wood Jr. is a Libra, Tim Burton's movie, "Ed Wood" is probably not a good fit.

## FIVE SUGGESTED MOVIES

**"Hamlet"** (1996)
Shakespeare's famous prince is the epitome of the vacillating Libra who wants to do the right thing, the just thing, but just can't make up his mind on how to go about it. There are several versions, of course, ranging from Laurence Olivier's to Mel Gibson's. But Libras will be happiest with Kenneth Branagh's because, well, it's the prettiest. Along with using almost every inch of the Bard's iambic pentameter (the movie is almost four hours long), Branagh takes his "Hamlet" out of its traditional setting — the brooding crags of medieval Denmark — and places it in a glittering nineteenth-century palace (Blenheim Palace, to be exact) filled with courtiers decked out in Ruritanian finery. Libra heaven.

### "Impromptu" (1991)

Beautiful settings, beautiful people and beautiful music (all right up Libra's alley), are the main attractions of James Lapine's hugely entertaining, impishly theatrical film. A romantic comedy playing dress-up, the movie gives us a gaggle of nineteenth-century celebs dropping bon mots about art, money and each other. Novelist George Sand, composers Frederic Chopin (Hugh Grant) and Franz Liszt (Julian Sands), and the poet Alfred de Musset (Mandy Patinkin) are among those gathered for a weekend in the country that would give Ingmar Bergman a summer night's smile. Nobody chews the scenery — the movie has Libra's sense of proportion — but almost everyone savors it. And rightly so.

### "To Kill a Mockingbird" (1962)

Gregory Peck won a much-deserved (and much-applauded) Oscar for his portrayal of Atticus Finch, the Lincoln-esque lawyer and widower raising his two children in small-town Alabama in the 1930s. Though redolent of early '60s liberalism, the film's simple dignity and unwavering humanity, along with its deeply held sense of right and wrong, remain untainted by time (as does Harper Lee's book). Libras will respond to the way the picture supports a firm belief in justice without resorting to zealotry. Peck must be one of the most measured, thoughtful crusaders the movies have ever given us. And he looks splendid in a white suit.

### "Sense and Sensibility" (1995)

Yes, it's more pretty people in pretty settings, but the focus here is balance, a theme dear to all Libras. Emma Thompson (who also wrote the Oscar-winning screenplay) and Kate Winslet costar as two penniless sisters trying to make their way among the sensible and senseless in late eighteenth-century England. Winslet, the passionate younger sister, must learn to use her head as well as her heart, while Thompson must learn to allow a little heart-smarts to creep into her head. Director Ang Lee distills every bit of intelligence, humor and romance from Jane Austen's novel, while giving an abrupt departure or secret engagement the same jaw-dropping impact as a hungry T-Rex.

### "A Hard Day's Night" (1964)

The Beatles first movie (John Lennon was a Libra) offers the Libra-friendly pleasures of a pure lark. There's not a pretentious thought in this picture's head (another Libra inducement). Rather, it pretends to be a semidocumentary look at what it might've been like to be John, Paul, George and/or Ringo in the earliest days of mop-top madness. Much like many Libras, the movie is endlessly upbeat and eager to please. And while some of director Richard Lester's high-spirited camera gimmicks — jump-cuts, fast-motion, etc. — may seem dated in a "psychedelic baby!" way, the movie still makes you want to twist and shout and scream and laugh and never, ever leave 1964.

## SIX TALENTED LIBRAS

### Jim Henson (September 24, 1936)

Henson is the one with the official Libra birthday, but it's his famous felt alter-ego, Kermit the Frog, who totally embodies so many Libra traits. Though Kermit has had his share of crosses to bear (remember, it isn't easy being green), his unfailingly pleasant outlook and rainbow-hued optimism make him an excellent example of Libra's balance and buoyancy. Of course he also suffers from Libra's unwillingness to make enemies, thus his long-standing and long-suffering relationship with Miss Piggy (a born Scorpio if ever there was one). As for those vaunted Libra good looks, well, he is a darn good-looking amphibian.

**Suggested Rental:** "The Muppet Movie" (1979)
"Sort of approximately" how Kermit the Frog, Miss Piggy, Fozzie Bear and all the rest of Henson's cloth clowns made it to Hollywood and signed the standard rich-and-famous contract. Thanks to Henson's (and company's) magic, the Muppets leave their studio and head out into the great outdoors (in one sequence, Kermit rides a bike!). With cameos by everyone from Steve Martin and Richard Pryor to Mel Brooks and Orson Welles, Henson's dog-and-pony show (or would that be frog-and-piggy show?) is definitely not just for kids or "Sesame Street" nostalgia freaks. What makes "The Muppet Movie" especially appealing to Libras is its upbeat outlook and graceful, giggly good humor.

**Libra Moment:** The opening scene sets the movie's tone with Kermit (or Kermie, as Miss Piggy likes to call him) plucking a banjo and singing "The Rainbow Connection" in his swamp home. The amiable optimist making his point through music is very Libra.

## Marcello Mastroianni

(September 28, 1924)
With his world-weary face and little-boy charm, Mastroianni was a Latin lover for the post-neorealist cinema. He was eternally Italian, with his taste for fine wine and fine women, for dining out and sleeping in. Yet his laid-back, sometimes befuddled, sometimes bemused macho appeal — memorably showcased in such early collaborations with Federico Fellini as "La Dolce Vita" and "8½" — struck a universal chord. In interviews, he was always lingering over pasta or coffee or a glass of wine. In movies, he was always lingering over Sophia Loren. He made life look pleasurable, and he made pleasure look respectable — a truly Libra gift.

**Suggested Rental:** "Dark Eyes" (1987)
The title supposedly refers to the film's heroine, a fragile Russian aristocrat extracted from a Chekov short story. But the eyes that dominate this lovely, bittersweet tragicomedy are Mastroianni's; they are the moist, pleading, self-deluding spaniel eyes of a buffoonish wastrel who botches his one chance at happiness. The star plays a once-promising architect who married rich and wasted his life on petty affairs. Then, at a spa, he meets the titular Russian lady, and what he thinks will be another meaningless fling becomes a potentially life-altering romantic obsession. For Libras, the movie's theme of taking action in life – and in love – will strike an especially meaningful chord.

**Libra Moment:** The screenplay was written by an old friend of Mastroianni's who, the star admitted, knew him all too well. Describing the character to an interviewer, the actor could just as easily have been describing one aspect of his own Libra self: "He's somebody with constant fantasies, really a superficial person. He's not a bad man, but he's so indecisive he has to fail." Libras, take heed.

## Julie Andrews (October 10, 1935)

She entered the movies as the chipper nanny in "Mary Poppins" and as the endlessly cheerful nun/governess in "The Sound of Music." Thus, one of our most talented singer-actors became forever typecast as wholesomeness incarnate. Not even baring her breasts in "S.O.B." or impersonating a man impersonating a drag queen in "Victor/Victoria" (both directed by her husband, Blake Edwards) could alter her squeaky clean image. Like many Libras, she's not nearly the icon of sweetness and light that she appears to be; underneath, there's a tart, intelligent woman. A fine actress, too, even when she's not seducing us with that five-octave voice.

**Suggested Rental:** "The Sound of Music" (1965)
Bashing this tale of the Von Trapp Family Singers has become
almost de rigeur, as if movie-lovers are ashamed to think they
were ever that sunnily innocent. But ironic hindsight can't
erase the fact that, when it came out, it was so phenomenally popular it was nicknamed "The Sound of Money." Plus,
let's not forget that it was based on a true story; the Von
Trapps really did have to "Climb Every Mountain" – well, at
least those between Austria and Switzerland – to escape the
Nazis. Loaded with saccaharine, yes, but music-loving Libras
will hum along happily with the justly famous Rodgers and
Hammerstein score. And Andrews doesn't hit a false note in
her acting or her singing as the fun nun.

**Libra Moment:** Director Robert Wise was totally surprised by
the movie's popularity. He later admitted, "I wasn't trying to
say a damn thing in the movie . . . but people just feel good
when they see it. There's a sense of warmth, of well-being, of
happiness and joy." Being a Libra, those things came naturally to Wise; they're a lot harder to come by for the rest of us.

## Charlton Heston (October 4, 1924)

If we're going to talk Libra ideals of justice
and statesmanship, then we may as well talk
Moses, a.k.a., Charlton Heston. A certified
hunk for decades, with his majestic profile
and epic-ready physique, the star has long
been a stunning example of Libra's rivetting good looks. And
before his post-'60s move into gung-ho conservatism, he was
an able spokesman for Libra moderation and fairness. There's
a gravity to Heston, a Libra need to weigh things carefully
before committing himself, in action or word. Principles and
conviction come easily to him; tenderness and ambiguity are
harder. Still, grounded sanity is one of the things Libras do
best when they're at their best.

**Suggested Rental:** "Ben-Hur" (1959)

It may not be the greatest movie ever made but, to date, it and 1997's "Titanic" are coholders of the record for winning the most Oscars (eleven, including Best Picture, Best Director and Best Actor). And while much of it plays like an illustrated Sunday school lesson, it's easily the best of the religous epics that were so popular in the '50s and '60s. Pluses include Heston's robust performance as the Jew who defies the Roman Empire and finds Christ; William Wyler's astute direction; and, best of all, that awesome chariot race. Libras will appreciate the movie's innate craftmanship, its well-honed balance between spectacle and the story's quasi-religious/humanistic themes.

**Libra Moment:** Heston, a team player like most Libras, worked hard to learn to drive a chariot for the climactic race. But, as filming grew closer, he expressed his doubts about his charioteering to expert stuntman Yakima Canutt, who taught him to drive and was staging the race. Canutt replied, "Chuck, just make sure you stay in the chariot. I guarantee you're gonna win the damn race." Not exactly Libran fair play, but a sane and balanced approach to movie make-believe.

## Susan Sarandon (October 4, 1946)

After a decade of well-acted but, well, forgettable ingenues, she caught our attention (and Burt Lancaster's) in "Atlantic City." Since then, she's won an Oscar ("Dead Man Walking"), had three kids while staying happily unmarried to Tim Robbins, and created a string of memorable roles in movies like "Bull Durham," "Thelma & Louise" and "Lorenzo's Oil." Sarandon's career could serve as a model for Libras at their best; she could've coasted by on her beauty but instead chose to let her sense of justice guide her both on-screen and off. Remember the Oscar night when she and copresenter Robbins spoke up for Haitians with AIDS? Two Libras at their strongest (he was born October 16).

**Suggested Rental:** "Thelma and Louise" (1991)
In the best desperado movie since Butch Cassidy met the Sundance Kid, Sarandon and Geena Davis (both Oscar nominees) play a waitress and a housewife who go on a weekend trip to get away from their dishwater-dull lives. But after an ill-fated stop at a roadside honky-tonk, they're on the lam, wanted by cops (led by Harvey Keitel) in three states. Essentially a road movie with feminist undertones, the film is exhuberant, raucously funny, provocative, and incredibly sure-footed, as our heroines learn to handle things with a resounding bang, not a girlish simper. Libras will applaud the film's unrelenting sense of fair play, as well as appreciate how glamorous jeans and t-shirts can look, with the right fashion touch.

**Libra Moment:** Director Ridley Scott didn't seem a likely choice for "Thelma and Louise" since he wasn't generally considered the kind of guy in touch with his feminine side. So a lot of interviewers wondered if he truly understood women. Sarandon had the perfect in-balance Libra answer: "I think it came out a lot better because he was at one end and I was at the other. Had it been a woman director out to make a feminist film, it probably would've been a little boring and maybe heavy handed and not as cavalier. It's good to have checks and balances."

## Jeff Goldblum (October 22, 1952)

He can be quirky and mannered, but there's an essential sanity about Jeff Goldblum, whether he's chasing flying saucers in "Independence Day" or being chased by a T-Rex in "Jurassic Park" and "The Lost World."
What comes across most about Goldblum, aside from his lanky,

off-beat good looks, is a sense that he's a good guy to have around. Even when he's playing a bad guy ("Deep Cover"), an irritating guy ("The Big Chill"), a decomposing guy ("The Fly") or a slightly goofy guy (just about everything else). Libra's charm and pleasant outlook crossed with Jewish angst have made him the most relaxed neurotic in movies. And he's got the paychecks to prove it.

**Suggested Rental:** "Jurassic Park" (1993)
Steven Spielberg's spectacular dinosaur extravaganza has Raptors and Brachiosaurs and more "oh-my!" than any movie in recent memory. Goldblum is one of a team of experts — a mathmatician specializing in the chaos theory — sent to evaluate the theme park to end all theme parks: A place where living, breathing, eating dinosaurs cloned from DNA roam a faux-primordial compund. The cast, which includes Sam Neill, Laura Dern and Richard Attenborough, does fine in their sketchy parts. But let's face it: This movie isn't about people; it's about dinosaurs. Once they get past all the running and screaming, Libras will appreciate the implicit message: Don't mess around with the natural balance of things.

**Libra Moment:** When Spielberg began casting his movie, Goldblum was the first person he signed. The director called it "a no-brainer choice." Why? Probably because of Goldblum's Libra sense of proportion. That is, he brings an almost Zen attitude to a situation that's pretty bonkers. In the movie, Attenborough says of Goldblum's character, "You'll have to excuse Dr. Malcolm. He suffers from an excess of personality." So does Goldblum, in a balanced Libra way, of course.

# MOVIES "BORN" AS LIBRAS

| | |
|---|---|
| BIG NIGHT | TO DIE FOR |
| THAT THING YOU DO | GET SHORTY |

THE SHAWSHANK
REDEMPTION
THE RIVER WILD
THE JOY LUCK CLUB
SHORT CUTS
THE LAST OF THE MOHICANS
A RIVER RUNS THROUGH IT
LITTLE MAN TATE
AVALON

MILLER'S CROSSING
TO SLEEP WITH ANGER
THE FABULOUS BAKER BOYS
CRIMES AND
MISDEMEANORS
DANGEROUS LIAISONS
WHITE PALACE
THE FISHER KING
CANDYMAN

## OTHER FAMOUS LIBRAS

**SEPTEMBER 23**
Mary Kay Place (1947)
Romy Schneider (1938)
Colin Blakeley (1930)
Mickey Rooney (1920)
Marcel Dalio (1899)
Walter Pigeon (1897)

**SEPTEMBER 24**
Kevin Sorbo (1958)

**SEPTEMBER 25**
Michael Madsen (1958)
Christopher Reeve (1952)
Colin Friels (1952)
Mark Hamill (1951)
Michael Douglas (1944)
Juliet Prowse (1936)
Aldo Ray (1926)
Robert Bresson (1907)

**SEPTEMBER 26**
Linda Hamilton (1956)

Olivia Newton-John (1948)
Mary Beth Hurt (1948)
Patrick O'Neal (1927)
Edmund Gwenn (1975)

**SEPTEMBER 27**
Meat Loaf (1951)
Wilford Brimley (1934)
Arthur Penn (1922)
George Raft (1895)

*Gwyneth Paltrow*

**SEPTEMBER 28**
Gwyneth Paltrow (1973)
Janeanne Garofolo (1964)
Brigitte Bardot (1934)
Arnold Stang (1925)

Peter Finch (1916)

**SEPTEMBER 29**
Emily Lloyd (1970)
Madeline Kahn (1942)
Robert Benton (1932)
Anita Ekberg (1931)
Trevor Howard (1916)
Stanley Kramer (1913)
Michelangelo Antonioni
   (1912)
Virginia Bruce (1910)
Gene Autrey (1907)
Greer Garson (1903)

**SEPTEMBER 30**
Eric Stoltz (1961)
Jack Wild (1957)
Angie Dickinson (1931)
Deborah Kerr (1921)
Michael Powell (1905)

**OCTOBER 1**
Randy Quaid (1950)
Jean-Jacques Annaud (1943)
Stella Stevens (1936)
Richard Harris (1932)
George Peppard (1928)
Laurence Harvey (1928)
James Whitmore (1921)
Walter Matthau (1920)
Stanley Holloway (1890)

**OCTOBER 2**
Clive Barker (1952)
Lorraine Bracco (1955)

Sting (1951)
Moses Gunn (1929)
"Spanky" McFarland (1926)
Bud Abbott (1895)
Groucho Marx (1890)

*Neve Campbell*

**OCTOBER 3**
Neve Campbell (1973)
Leo McCarey (1911)
Warner Oland (1879)
Charles Middleton (1879)

**OCTOBER 4**
Alicia Silverstone (1976)
Armande Assante (1949)
Buster Keaton (1895)

**OCTOBER 5**
Kate Winslet (1975)
Guy Pearce (1967)
Karen Allen (1951)
Glynis Johns (1923)
Donald Pleasance (1919)
Joshua Logan (1908)
Larry Fine (1902)
Louis Lumiere (1864)

**OCTOBER 6**
Britt Ekland (1942)

Carole Lombard (1908)
Janet Gaynor (1906)
Mitchell Lieson (1898)

## OCTOBER 7
June Allyson (1917)
Alfred Drake (1914)
Andy Devine (1905)

*Sigourney Weaver*

## OCTOBER 8
Edward Zwick (1952)
Sigourney Weaver (1949)
Jean-Jacques Beineix (1946)
Chevy Chase (1943)
Paul Hogan (1939)
Klaus Kinski (1926)

*Chevy Chase*

## OCTOBER 9
Michael Pare (1959)
Tony Shalhoub (1953)
Robert Wuhl (1951)
Jacques Tati (1908)

## OCTOBER 10
Jessica Harper (1949)
Ben Vereen (1946)
Charles Dance (1946)
Peter Coyote (1942)
Ed Wood Jr. (1924)
Helen Hayes (1900)

## OCTOBER 11
Luke Perry (1966)
Joan Cusack (1962)
Ron Leibman (1937)

## OCTOBER 12
Kirk Cameron (1970)
Susan Anton (1950)

## OCTOBER 13
Kelly Preston (1965)
John Lone (1962)
Pamela Tiffin (1942)
Art Garfunkel (1941)
Yves Montand (1921)
Jack MacGowran (1918)
Robert Walker (1918)
Cornel Wilde (1915)

## OCTOBER 14
Carroll Ballard (1937)
Roger Moore (1927)
Allan Jones (1907)
Pert Kelton (1907)
Lillian Gish (1893)
Clarence Muse (1899)

## OCTOBER 15
Victor Banerjee (1956)
Tanya Roberts (1954)
Penny Marshall (1942)
Linda Lavin (1937)
Vittorio De Sca (1923)
Mervyn LeRoy (1900)
Ina Claire (1892)
Jane Darwell (1879)

## OCTOBER 16
Tim Robbins (1958)
David Zucker (1947)
Angela Lansbury (1925)

## OCTOBER 17
Sam Bottoms (1955)
Howard E. Rollins Jr. (1950)
Margot Kidder (1948)
Michael McKean (1947)
Linda Darnell (1923)
Montgomery Clift (1920)
Rita Hayworth (1918)
Jean Arthur (1900)
Elinor Glyn (1864)

## OCTOBER 18
Vincent Spano (1962)
Jean-Claude Van Damme
  (1960)
Joe Morton (1947)
Peter Boyle (1933)
George C. Scott (1927)
Melina Mercouri (1925)
Miriam Hopkins (1902)
Roy Del Ruth (1889)

## OCTOBER 19
Jon Favreau (1966)
John Lithgow (1945)
Divine (1945)
Simon Ward (1941)
Michael Gambon (1940)
Auguste Lumiere (1862)

## OCTOBER 20
Danny Boyle (1956)
Jerry Orbach (1935)
Jean-Pierre Melville (1917)
Arlene Francis (1908)
Rex Ingram (1895)
Bela Lugosi (1882)

## OCTOBER 21
Carrie Fisher (1956)

## OCTOBER 22
Lee Meredith (1947)
Catherine Deneuve (1943)
Annette Funicello (1942)
Tony Roberts (1939)
Christopher Lloyd (1938)
Derek Jacobi (1938)
Joan Fontaine (1920)
Constance Bennett (1905)

# SCORPIO

## OCTOBER 23 — NOVEMBER 21

For centuries, Scorpios have been renowned as the sexiest sign in the zodiac.

Hmm, can't imagine what use that would be in Hollywood . . .

They are as ego-ridden as Leos but without Leo's sunny radiance. Rather, it is a dark sign — some have even called it malevolent. The flip side of Scorpio's difficult reputation is derived from its alternate symbol, the Eagle. Scorpios sting, but they can soar as well. Power-hungry, shrewd, determined and secretive, they are well equipped for the byzantine intrigues of Hollywood.

Oh, and there's that sex thing.

Leading-men Scorpios range from Richard Dreyfuss to Richard Burton, from Sam Waterston to Charles Bronson. Matthew McConaughey, Burt Lancaster, Ethan Hawke and Leonardo DiCaprio also are magnetic Scorpios.

Their leading ladies include such sexy beauties as Julia Roberts, Vivien Leigh, Meg Ryan, Veronica Lake, Grace Kelly, Winona Ryder and Dorothy Dandridge. And to prove that beauty isn't just skin-deep, try Jodie Foster, Sally Field, Demi Moore and Goldie Hawn, determined Scorpio women who've produced their own films.

While Scorpios enjoy the limelight, they're at their best slightly outside it. Thus, they make excellent and memorable supporting players: F. Murray Abraham, Claude Rains, Ruth Gordon, Bob Hoskins, Jack Elam, Delroy Lindo, Danny De Vito. And of course, all that need for manipulation and control makes them natural directors: Martin Scorsese, Mike Nichols, Ang Lee, Sam Raimi, Don Siegel, Roland Emmerich.

Scorpio movie-lovers prefer a sting in their films. A little darkness doesn't hurt, either. In fact, the entire film noir genre could've been made for Scorpios. Generally, they just aren't "Sound of Music" kind of folk, and you're probably not going to find many Scorpios lingering over old Shirley Temple flicks.

## FIVE SUGGESTED SCORPIO RENTALS

**"Richard III"** (1995)
The Laurence Olivier version from the '50s is excellent, but there's more of Scorpio's cunning sting in this version starring Ian McKellan and directed by Richard Loncraine. They've transferred Shakespeare's tale of humpbacked Richard of Gloucester to England in the 1930s. After a lengthy civil war, Richard's brother has been crowned. As we learn in the famous "winter of our discontent" speech, which begins as a coronation toast in a ballroom and ends as a cynical confession in the men's room, Richard has his own designs on the throne. The cast is a who's who of England's best (along with Americans Annette Bening and Robert

Downey Jr.) but the crown jewel is McKellan's magnificent, media-savvy monster, as unctuous as he is unrepentant. Surely the real Richard had Scorpio somewhere in his horoscope. Or maybe just Scorpio Rising?

### "Blue Velvet" (1986)

Remember that self-destructive, obsessive side of Scorpio? Remember that sex thing? David Lynch burned a hole in our cinematic psyche with this brilliantly disturbing film. He takes us for a walk on the wild side of "See Spot Run" America via a disquieting murder mystery/love story, starring Kyle McLachlan and Laura Dern as two innocents staking out a mysterious chanteuse (Isabella Rossellini). What begins as a lark turns into a nightmare, as they're plunged into a netherworld of sex, violence and unbridled evil. And Dennis Hopper. This is a frightening, shocking and, at times, blackly comic film, crafted by one of the most original minds in movies. Lynch serves up loss of innocence and the malignancy of chaos with a "golly-gee" tone, "omigosh!" visuals and demonically disturbing events. Some people won't get it. Scorpios will.

### "Surviving Picasso" (1996)

Think of it as a portrait of the artist as a not-very-young Scorpio. Neither a full-blown study of Picasso (born October 25) or a clichéd treatise on "Abusive Famous Men and the Women Who Love Them," this bravura film is something of a distillation: A look at the legendary painter (Anthony Hopkins) through the eyes of Francoise Gilot (Natascha McAlhone), the only woman who left him before he left her (however, veteran scene-stealer, Julianne Moore, is far more vital as a former mistress). Hopkins makes Picasso a sacred monster, portraying his genius as unfettered appetite, devouring everyone and everything in its path. He's a visionary/predator, with Scorpio's vitality, sexuality and devilish ingenuity for manipulation and torment.

Sure, genius has its privileges, but not all geniuses choose to express them in such a purely Scorpio manner.

### "Diabolique" (1955)

For a good laugh, rent the Sharon Stone/Isabelle Adjani remake. But for a good scare — and a tingle on the back of your neck that just won't quit — you want the original, directed by the great Henri-Georges Clouzot (a fellow Scorpio). In a run-down French boarding school, a strong-minded mistress (Simone Signoret) and a weak-willed wife (Vera Clouzot — yes, the director's wife) conspire to murder the man they share — and despise. He's the school's head-master, a sadistic petty tyrant who's managed to mistreat both the women in his life. A triumph of atmosphere, character, diabolical wit and outright scare-you-silly shock tactics, the movie's has Scorpio's cool appreciation for schemes and counterschemes. And the world of bitterness and recrimination created by Clouzot is one Scorpios will find familiar. Perhaps a bit too familiar.

### "Out of the Past" (1946)

There are dozens and dozens of film noirs that would suit Scorpios, but this one is directed by Jacques Tourneur, another excellent filmmaker born under this sign. Robert Mitchum plays the ill-fated hero, cynical and sexy, and Jane Greer is the femme fatale, sultry and smart, he's sent to track down. Full of elusive, threatening shadows, insinuating swirls of cigarette smoke and rain-lashed streets, the movie creates a mood of camera-angled alienation and inchoate dread. It's a dark world of corruption and deception, of . . . well, are we talking a Scorpio kind of movie or what? But be prepared for a possible paranoia hangover. And you won't be able to get the dialogue out of your head. Sample exchange: Greer simpers to Mitchum, "I don't want to die," and he replies, "Neither do I, but if I do, I wanna die last."

## SIX FAMOUS SCORPIOS

**Julia Roberts** (October 28, 1967)
She initially seems too much the beaming, brown-eyed girl to be a Scorpio. In fact, her brother Eric — intense, dark, brooding — would seem to be the true Scorpio in the family (he's an Aries). But underneath the  delicious giggle and the waifish beauty are hints of a far more complex personality — witness her headline-making private life (marrying Lyle Lovett, not marrying Kiefer Sutherland). It takes a Scorpio's steeliness to survive that kind of tabloid maelstrom. And only a Scorpio could turn an L.A. hooker into America's sweetheart, as she did in "Pretty Woman." Now, that's sex appeal. Her post–"Pretty Woman" roles haven't been as successful, but they reflect her Scorpio love of detection and secrets. Consider these roles: a snoopy reporter in "I Love Trouble;" a snoopy law student in "The Pelican Brief;" a snoopy assistant district attorney in "Conspiracy Theory;" and even a snoopy chambermaid in "Mary Reilly."

**Suggested Rental:** "My Best Friend's Wedding" (1997)
No one could believe that sweet, adorable Julia Roberts would play a scheming, manipulative bitch out to ruin a wedding and steal the groom for herself. But she does — and she does it beautifully in this surprise hit that helped put her career back on track. As Julianne Potter, a Manhattan food critic, she shows up at her longtime best pal's (fellow Scorpio, Dermot Mulroney) wedding and immediately decides that her feelings for him are, well, more than friendly. Cameron Diaz is the fiancee still very much in the way, while Rupert Everett almost steals the movie as Potter's gay best friend who briefly poses as her fiance. But he can't quite take it away from Roberts, who remains front and center with her smartly comic performance. She even manages to make her character's self-destructive ruthlessness funny while daring to add a caustic touch of Scorpio obsessiveness.

**Scorpio Moment:** Playing not-so-nice while looking absolutely fabulous is a balancing act only a Scorpio would think of — and pull off. Pumping for the movie at a convention of movie-theater owners before it was released, Roberts did some career-assessing and mock-pleaded with them: "My hair is a lovely shade of red and very long and curly the way you guys like it; for the love of God, please see this movie!"

## Vivien Leigh (November 5, 1913)

Atlanta (actually, the jungle set from "King Kong") was in flames the night a demure English actress claimed her rightful place in cinema history as Scarlett O'Hara. And befitting her fiery introduction to immortality, her star shone briefly but oh-so-brightly. She was one half of one of the most famous showbiz marriages ever — to Laurence Olivier — and its ultimate failure probably contributed to her emotional ill-health and early death (at age fifty-three). She didn't make many movies, preferring England and the stage to Hollywood, but when she did, she made an impact. "Gone With the Wind" won her her first Oscar. Over a decade later, she won her second as another Southern belle — the faded desperate Blanche in "A Streetcar Named Desire." In an eerie way, Blanche could be Scarlett, later in life and unlucky in love, trying to survive on plantation dreams and strategies as flimsy as paper lanterns.

**Suggested Rental:** "Gone With the Wind" (1939)
Well, why not? It's one of the most celebrated movies ever made, and, while film buffs may have differing opinions on its true place in the cinematic pantheon, what everyone does agree on is that it represents the apogee of the Hollywood studio system during its Golden Age. Plus, it won eight Oscars, so somebody liked it. The legendary cast has become forever melded with their characters: Clark Gable as Rhett,

Leslie Howard as Ashley, Olivia de Havilland as Melanie and Hattie McDaniel as Mammy. And most of all, Leigh as Scarlett. As Margaret Mitchell's unstoppable heroine, Leigh is astonishingly good as a green-eyed vixen with a CEO's drive and a carpetbagger's cunning. No telling what Scarlett's sign is — Margaret Mitchell didn't go in for those sort of details — but Scarlett's shrewdness and sexual magnetism, her determination and survival instincts all suggest Scorpio.

**Scorpio Moment:** Director George Cukor was abruptly dismissed only two weeks into filming. One theory was that Clark Gable was wary of his reputation as a "women's director." Another was that David O. Selznick didn't want anyone else leaving their mark on his movie. Leigh was horrifed when she heard, but reacted with a Scorpio's tactical skill. Unbeknownst to Selznick, she began visiting Cukor in secret to work on her scenes. Scarlett herself couldn't have handled the situation better.

### Richard Burton (November 10, 1925)

The line on Burton was always that he sold out, that the heir apparent to Olivier and Gielgud renounced his crown for Hollywood's bright lights, big bucks and, of course, that woman — Elizabeth Taylor. But even if he did trade Shakespeare for champagne and cleavage, his talent was undeniable. So was his Scorpio sex appeal, despite his pock-marked face and later boozy bloat. For even if the body was ravaged, there was still that voice, the one that made you think, gee, the Angel Gabriel must sound like that. As is sadly often true of Scorpios, Burton was prone to addictions — first the alcohol, then Taylor, then the Liz-and-Dick Show. If he seemed to squander his talent more than others, perhaps it's because he had so much to toy with. And if his decline seemed darker than others, maybe it's because we remember him best bathed in the radiance of a thousand flashbulbs.

**Suggested Rental:** "Who's Afraid of Virginia Woolf?" (1966) Taylor won the Oscar (deservedly so), but Burton gives the better performance in this searing version of Edward Albee's prize-winning play. He's George, the down-trodden, seemingly weak college professor locked in a till-death-do-us-part-or-we-kill-each-other marriage with Martha, the vulgar, shrewish daughter of the college's president. The movie follows the two through a very long night they spend with a young couple — a new faculty member and his wife (George Segal and Sandy Dennis) — they've invited over for Fun 'n' Games (including "Get the Guests" and "Hump the Hostess"). By daylight, however, the worm has turned, and George unleashes a Scorpio sting that's devastating. What's even more Scorpion-like is the film's relentless grudge-holding. George and Martha don't forget a slight, no matter how ancient, and they store up their venom for just the right strike.

**Scorpio Moment:** When the time came to shoot one of the film's most difficult scenes, Burton tried to postpone it, saying he wanted to visit with his stepsons before they went back to boarding school. The producer refused, but they later found Burton in his dressing room in tears. He didn't need to see the boys; he just couldn't do the scene that night. Director Mike Nichols, himself a Scorpio, understood: "Richard had black days. It's as simple as that. During the production, he had perhaps eight or ten of them . . . and how can you tell him he's being a schmuck when he's telling you he's so untalented and hopeless?" Nobody has blacker days than Scorpios.

## Whoopi Goldberg (November 13, 1949)

You never know what she's thinking but you always know she's thinking. Whether hosting the Oscars, hanging out with "Comic Relief" cofounders Billy Crystal and Robin Williams, or getting serious in such fine films as "The Long

Walk Home," "Sarafina!" and "Corrina, Corrina," Whoopi radiates Scorpio smarts. The gears are always turning — just like her career, which has gone up and down at least a half-dozen times since she made her film debut in 1985's "The Color Purple." Whoopi has Scorpio's endurance — she's in it for the long haul — and Scorpio's willingness to break through barriers. She's become a star despite her race (roles for African-American women are scarce), her non-traditional looks and her outspokenness. Whoopi monitors her sting, but she never censors it. She'll work with the system, but when it's wrong, watch out.

**Suggested Rental:** "Ghost" (1990)
As the storefront psychic who can't believe she's talking to a dead white boy (Patrick Swayze), Whoopi stole the movie, won a Best Supporting Actress Oscar and saved her career (again). Fellow Scorpio Demi Moore plays Swayze's distraught, loving wife. (Remember her and that pottery wheel? Remember what we said about sexy Scorpio?) Early in the movie, he's murdered, but his spirit returns in an attempt to protect Moore from the bad guys who did him in (turns out that a friend of the couple was behind it; Scorpios always have had a weakness for the wrong loyalties). Whoopi's character becomes the unlikely medium for Swayze's messages. Some of the film is pure hokum (especially near the end), but like cheap wine, cheap sentiment can be awfully potent. This weepie has class and confidence, and it isn't even afraid to send its hero into a '40s movie haze of twinkling heavenly lights.

**Scorpio Moment:** Whoopi was the first African-American woman to win an Oscar since Hattie McDaniel won in 1939 for "Gone With the Wind." And she won it for a role that the producers agonized over for six months before giving it to her. Not only was she an unusual choice (for all the reasons cited above), but her career was in one of its major downswings. However, Scorpios have a natural affinity for the occult, and when she read the script, she knew she had to play the pseudo-seer because "it was the best part in the movie." She must be . . . psychic?

## Martin Scorsese (November 17, 1942)

He is probably the best American director never to win an Oscar (not yet, anyway). He is also, as befits a Scorpio, intense, obsessive and totally dedicated to the cinema (some of his most important work has been in restoration and preservation). His best films – "Mean Streets," "Taxi Driver," "The King of Comedy," "Raging Bull," New York, New York" and "GoodFellas" – all evince some form of the Scorsese jitters. His Scorpio fascination with mysticism and the occult shows up in a more respectable guise as his fascination with growing up devoutly Catholic in New York's Little Italy. He once said, "My whole life has been movies and religion. That's it. Nothing else." Apparently, if you're Martin Scorsese, nothing else is needed. He is a film fantasist and film fanatic, as well as a film buff and film genius.

**Suggested Rental:** "Taxi Driver" (1976)
"Are you talking to me?" That's what New York cabbie, Travis Bickle (Robert De Niro), snarls into his mirror as he edges ever closer to going over the edge. As it turned out, this remarkable movie talked to a lot of people. Its theme of alienation and loneliness leading to frustration and unbalanced anger (and finally to madness and even murder) seemed to sum up our country's collective post-'60s hangover. The extraordinary supporting cast mixes Harvey Keitel (the most evil pimp you'll ever see) and Jodie Foster (the most disturbing Lolita-prostitute you'll ever see) with Cybill Shepherd (playing it very straight) and Albert Brooks (playing it as straight as he can). But the central relationship is between the filmmaker and his star; Scorsese directs De Niro with the assurance of a weapons expert aiming a loaded pistol.

**Scorpio Moment:** Just spending time inside Travis Bickle's head is a kind of Scorpio moment. But even before a single frame was shot, Scorsese admitted that he wasn't thinking so much about a crazed taxi driver in Manhattan. Rather, as he told an interviewer, "I'd always wanted to do a movie of Dostoyevsky's 'Notes From the Underground,' and that's what 'Taxi Driver' is." Scorsese probably didn't know it at the time, but Dostoyevsky is a Scorpio (October 30). One Scorpio's darkness overlaying another's.

## Jodie Foster (November 19, 1962)

She brings to the table her Scorpio intensity and magnetism. And one more thing – Scorpio's mystery. She's been acting for us since she was ten (actually, she made her public debut as a tyke in one of those bare-bottomed Coppertone ads). Yet, aside from her tremendous talent and intelligence, we don't really know her, which suits her just fine. As a child actress, her breakthrough role came in "Taxi Driver;" she flaunted a precocious sexuality as the pretty-baby prostitute. As an adult, she weathered some rough years and a string of unremarkable films before coming into her Oscar-winning own with "The Accused" and "The Silence of the Lambs." Her role as the dogged scientist in "Contact" is a perfect reflection of her Scorpio affinity for otherworldliness (in this case, extraterrestrials), as well as for a kind of determination that bordered on obsession.

**Suggested Rental:** "The Silence of the Lambs" (1992)
Jonathan Demme's sensational adaptation of Thomas Harris' chilling best-seller brought Foster her second Oscar before she turned thirty. She plays Clarice Starling, an inexperienced FBI trainee who tries to catch one serial killer, a monster who skins his female victims, by interviewing another serial killer – the perversely brilliant Dr. Hannibal Lecter (Anthony

Hopkins). He's also known as "Hannibal the Cannibal" (for reasons that become frighteningly clear midmovie). Lecter is a smiling psycho, as lethally appealing as he is mind-bendingly frightening. The interplay between the two provides some of the most memorable moments in movie history. Yet, while Hopkins's character is initially the most Scorpio-like — with his poisonous pseudo-flattery and mocking insinuation — he somehow brings out the Scorpio side in Clarice. She loses her innocence and gains his guile. And, perhaps, his sting.

**Scorpio Moment:** The detective, the resolver of mysteries, is an appealing one for Scorpios, and it obviously appealed to Foster who did her own detective work in city morgues and police training centers to prepare for the role. However, Demme originally wanted Michelle Pfeiffer, so Foster sent him a good-sport, may-I-be-your-second-choice note. Then Demme discovered that his first choice was "unable to come to terms with the overpowering darkness of the piece." Of course, what disturbed Pfeiffer intrigued Foster. After all, darkness is what Scorpios are all about.

## MOVIES "BORN" AS SCORPIOS

MR. SMITH GOES TO
 WASHINGTON
STEEL MAGNOLIAS
DRUGSTORE COWBOY
JACOB'S LADDER
HOME ALONE
DANCES WITH WOLVES
THE ADDAMS FAMILY
RESERVOIR DOGS
PERSUASION
LEAVING LAS VEGAS

MICHAEL COLLINS
JUDE
THE ENGLISH PATIENT
FAIRY TALE
THE ICE STORM
THE WINGS OF THE DOVE
EVE'S BAYOU
THE RAINMAKER
THE AMERICAN PRESIDENT
INTERVIEW WITH THE
 VAMPIRE

# OTHER FAMOUS SCORPIOS

**OCTOBER 23**
Sam Raimi (1959)
Ang Lee (1954)
Philip Kaufman (1936)
Bella Darvi (1928)
Coleen Gray (1922)

**OCTOBER 24**
B. D.Wong (1962)
Kevin Kline (1947)
F. Murray Abraham (1939)
Jackie Coogan (1914)
Jack Warner (1896)

**OCTOBER 25**
Gayle Anne Hurd (1955)
Billy Barty (1924)
Leo G. Carroll (1892)
Abel Gance (1889)

**OCTOBER 26**
Dylan McDermott (1962)
Cary Elwes (1962)
Bob Hoskins (1942)
Ralph Bashki (1938)
Baby Peggy (1918)
Don Siegel (1912)
H.B. Warner (1875)

**OCTOBER 27**
Peter Firth (1953)
Roberto Benigni (1952)
Ivan Reitman (1946)
John Cleese (1939)

Jean-Pierre Cassel (1932)
Ruby Dee (1924)
Teresa Wright (1918)

**OCTOBER 28**
Joaquin Phoenix (1974)
Jami Gertz (1965)
Daphne Zuniga (1963)
Lauren Holly (1963)
Dennis Franz (1944)
Annie Potts (1952)
Michael Crichton (1942)
Jane Alexander (1939)
Joan Plowright (1929)
Elsa Lanchester (1902)
Edith Head (1898)

*Winona Ryder*

**OCTOBER 29**
Winona Ryder (1971)
Joely Fisher (1965)
Kate Jackson (1948)
Richard Dreyfuss (1947)
Peter Watkins (1935)
Eddie Constantine (1915)
Akim Tamiroff (1899)

**OCTOBER 30**
Nia Long (1970)
Kevin Pollak (1958)
Charles Martin Smith (1953)
Harry Hamlin (1951)
Henry Winkler (1945)
Ed Lauter (1940)
Claude Lelouch (1937)
Louis Malle (1932)
Nestor Almendros (1930)
Ruth Gordon (1896)

**OCTOBER 31**
Dermot Mulroney (1963)
Ken Wahl (1960)
John Candy (1950)
Sally Kirkland (1944)
David Ogden Stiers (1942)
Michael Landon (1936)
Lee Grant (1927)
Barbara Bel Geddes (1922)
Dale Evans (1912)
Ethel Waters (1896)

**NOVEMBER 1**
Toni Collette (1972)
Rachel Ticotin (1958)
Jeannie Berlin (1949)
Edward Van Sloan (1881)

**NOVEMBER 2**
Stephane Audran (1932)
Ann Rutherford (1920)
Burt Lancaster (1913)
Luchino Visconti (1906)
James Dunn (1905)

Paul Ford (1901)
Alice Brady (1892)

**NOVEMBER 3**
Dolph Lundgren (1959)
Kate Capshaw (1953)
Dennis Miller (1953)
Roseanne (1952)
Lulu (1946)
Jeremy Brett (1933)
Monica Vitti (1931)
John Barry (1933)
Lois Smith (1930)
Charles Bronson (1921)

*Matthew McCanaughey*

**NOVEMBER 4**
Matthew McCanaughey
 (1969)
Ralph Macchio (1961)
Martin Balsam (1919)
Art Carney (1918)
Cameron Mitchell (1918)
Gig Young (1913)
Will Rogers (1879)

**NOVEMBER 5**
Tatum O'Neal (1963)
Sam Shepard (1943)
Elke Sommer (1940)

Harris Yulin (1937)
Herb Edelman (1933)
Roy Rogers (1912)
Joel McCrea (1905)

## NOVEMBER 6
Ethan Hawke (1970)
Brad Davis (1949)
Nigel Havers (1949)
Sally Field (1946)
Mike Nichols (1931)
Francis Lederer (1906)
Thomas H. Ince (1882)

## NOVEMBER 7
Lindsay Duncan (1950)
Barry Newman (1938)
Dean Jagger (1905)

## NOVEMBER 8
Parker Posey (1968)
Alfre Woodard (1953)
Alain Delon (1935)
Darla Hood (1931)
Paolo Taviani (1931)
Esther Rolle (1924)
Gene Saks (1921)
June Havoc (1916)
Robert Strauss (1913)
Marie Prevost (1898)

## NOVEMBER 9
Bille August (1948)
Dorothy Dandridge (1923)
Hedy Lamarr (1913)
Kay Thompson (1913)

Mae Marsh (1895)
Ed Wynn (1886)
Edna Mae Oliver (1883)
Marie Dressler (1869)

## NOVEMBER 10
Roland Emmerich (1955)
Ann Reinking (1949)
Albert Hall (1937)
Roy Scheider (1935)
Richard Burton (1925)
Harry Andrews (1911)
Claude Rains (1889)

*Leonardo DiCaprio*

## NOVEMBER 11
Leonardo DiCaprio (1974)
Demi Moore (1962)
Bibi Andersson (1935)
Stubby Kaye (1918)
Patric Knowles (1911)
Robert Ryan (1909)
Sam Spiegel (1903)
Pat O'Brien (1899)
Rene Clair (1898)
Roland Young (1887)

## NOVEMBER 12
David Schwimmer (1966)
Jonathan Nossiter (1961)

Patrice Leconte (1947)
Wallace Shawn (1943)
Ina Balin (1937)
Grace Kelly (1928)
Kim Hunter (1922)
Richard Quine (1920)
Jacques Tourneur (1904)
Jack Oakie (1903)

**NOVEMBER 13**
Joe Mantegna (1947)
Jean Seberg (1938)
Garry Marshall (1934)
Richard Mulligan (1932)
Linda Christian (1924)
Madeleine Sherwood (1922)
Oskar Werner (1922)
Jack Elam (1916)

**NOVEMBER 14**
Laura San Giacomo (1962)
D. B. Sweeney (1961)
Ray Sharkey (1952)
Veronica Lake (1922)
Brian Keith (1921)
Louise Brooks (1906)
Dick Powell (1904)

**NOVEMBER 15**
Beverly D'Angelo (1953)
Roger Donaldson (1943)
Sam Waterston (1940)
Yaphet Kotto (1937)
Joanna Barnes (1934)
Petula Clarke (1932)
John Kerr (1931)

Ed Asner (1929)
Francesco Rosi (1922)
Lewis Stone (1879)

**NOVEMBER 16**
Martha Plimpton (1970)
Lisa Blount (1967)
Allison Anders (1954)
Joanna Pettet (1944)
Royal Dano (1922)
Burgess Meredith (1907)
Mabel Normand (1894)

**NOVEMBER 17**
Sophie Marceau (1966)
RuPaul (1960)
Mary Elizabeth Mastrantonio
   (1958)
Roland Joffe (1945)
Danny De Vito (1944)
Lauren Hutton (1943)
Peter Cook (1937)
Rock Hudson (1925)
Lee Strasberg (1901)
Mischa Auer (1905)

**NOVEMBER 18**
Elizabeth Perkins (1960)
Sinbad (1956)
Delroy Lindo (1952)
David Hemmings (1941)
Brenda Vaccaro (1939)
Imogene Coca (1908)

**NOVEMBER 19**
Meg Ryan (1961)

Kathleen Quinlan (1954)
Robert Beltram (1953)
Ted Turner (1938)
Alan Young (1919)
Nancy Carroll (1904)
Clifton Webb (1891)

*Meg Ryan*

**NOVEMBER 20**
Sean Young (1959)
Bo Derek (1956)
Richard Masur (1948)
Veronica Hamel (1943)
Rex Reason (1928)
Estelle Parsons (1927)
Gene Tierney (1920)
Evelyn Keyes (1919)
Henri-Georges Clouzot (1907)
Reginald Denny (1891)
Robert Armstrong (1890)

**NOVEMBER 21**
Goldie Hawn (1945)
Harold Ramis (1944)
Juliet Mills (1941)
Laurence Luckinbill (1940)
Marlo Thomas (1938)
Vivian Blaine (1923)
Ralph Meeker (1920)
Eleanor Powell (1912)

# SAGITTARIUS

## NOVEMBER 22 — DECEMBER 21

Hollywood and happy-go-lucky Sagittarians are a natural match. Attractive, gregarious extroverts, they have a built-in resilience that enables them to bounce back from the myriad of disappointments that a movie career so often offers.

They have another advantage, too. Born under Jupiter, the planet of good fortune, Sagittarians are among the luckiest of all signs. And in a crap shoot like the movies, that's a plus.

As their symbol — the half-horse, half-man Centaur with a drawn bow — suggests, Sagittarians are natural athletes, and thus are easily able to express themselves through their bodies — or someone else's body. Choreographer Busbey Berkeley, famous for his looney-tunes dance extravaganzas in the '30s, is a Sag. So are daredevil leading men Douglas Fairbanks Jr. and Kirk Douglas; limber funny men Harpo Marx and Dick Van Dyke; stuntman extraordinaire Yakima Canutt; and martial arts superstar Bruce Lee.

But Sagittarians' physical prowess is matched — perhaps surpassed — by their extreme mental agility. That, combined with their surplus energy and that in-the-stars good luck, has made them some of the most creative and successful people in the business, including Steven Spielberg, Woody Allen, Walt Disney, Bette Midler, Jane Fonda, Georges Melies, Ridley Scott, Kenneth Branagh, Frank Sinatra and Edward G. Robinson.

The Sagittarian movie-lover is drawn to energy and humor. And any film that hopes to please a Sag better be on its toes mentally, too. No wonder screwball comedies like "The Lady Eve," "The Awful Truth" and "Bringing Up Baby" have Sagittarius written all over them. So do movies with a little swashbuckling dash (try "The Man in the Iron Mask," either version) Tear-jerkers bore Sags silly, and while the dark soul-searching of, say, an Ingmar Berman movie, may stimulate them mentally, they're just as likely to be thinking "get over it" long before the movie's over.

One interesting coincidence: Sag, the short-hand for Sagittarians, happens to be the acronym for the Screen Actors Guild (SAG). Coincidence . . . or in the stars?

## FIVE SUGGESTED SAGITTARIAN RENTALS

**"Bringing Up Baby"** (1938)
With their bright, chatty characters and battle of equals take on the battle of the sexes, screwball comedies are a natural for Sagittarians. This film, directed by Howard Hawks, pairs Katharine Hepburn and Cary Grant at their breezy best. Grant is a terribly smart, terribly absent-minded paleontologist devoted to his dinosaur bones. Hepburn is a whimsical, self-assured (to the point of irritating) heiress devoted to the pursuit of Grant. Baby is a leopard. Sags will savor the picture's crackling energy and the stars' crackling rapport (it helps that they're two of the

most gorgeous people ever to grace a movie screen). Like true Sags, Hepburn and Grant's characters are impulsive, high-spirited and don't really get the whole romance thing. And, like true Sags, they don't really care. They just naturally accept their Sagittarian good fortune: finding each other.

**"The Adventures of Baron Munchausen"** (1989)
Robin Williams's head literally spins in this grand phantasmagoria directed by Sagittarian Terry Gilliam. And so will yours. Cluttered, clamorous and rambunctious, this comic fantasy is an ecstatic wallow in sensory overload (ring any bells, Sags?). Based on the exploits of an eighteenth-century nobleman whose name is synonymous with exaggeration (like most Sags, he can't keep his mouth shut), the movie ricochets from the Arabian Nights to Greek mythology to the moon. At one point, Venus (Uma Thurman) literally dances on air with the Baron (John Neville). Sags love to travel, and this film certainly does that. But it's also a celebration of all the architects of artifice, the fabulists and tale-tellers. Gilliam set out to make a relentlessly active, wonder-filled film. And, bless his hyperactive soul, he succeeded.

**"Much Ado About Nothing"** (1993)
Kenneth Branagh (another Sagittarian) directs and costars with his then-wife, Emma Thompson. They play Benedick and Beatrice, Shakespeare's famously smart-mouthed pair who must be tricked into realizing that they're made for each other. Branagh has turned the Bard's romantic comedy into a Mediterranean holiday – a sexy, boisterous, sun-drenched Tuscan idyll (horse-loving Sags will relish the cavalry-is-coming intro of the male characters). The decidedly eclectic cast ranges from a noble Denzel Washington as Don Pedro to a malicious Keanu Reeves as Don John to Michael Keaton as a Beetlejuiced-up Dogberry. But Beatrice and Benedick hold center stage with their Sagittarian sparring and their Sagittarian refusal to be tied down, even by love. As Beatrice

says, "a star danced" when she was born. We can all guess which star in what constellation.

### "Sid and Nancy" (1986)

Here's a love story that goes Erich Segal one better: What can you say about a twenty-one-year-old rock star who overdosed a few months after allegedly stabbing to death his twenty-year-old girlfriend? You can say plenty according to Alex Cox (another Sag), director of this rudely sordid yet perversely captivating account of the eat-it-raw romance between Sid Vicious (Gary Oldman), of Sex Pistols fame, and his American groupie/sweetheart, Nancy Spungen (Chloe Webb). Less star-crossed than strung-out, this hard-rock Romeo and Juliet live in a world of puke, blood and broken needles. Yet theirs is also a peculiarly tender and comic tale of love among the ruined. The Sag connection? Well, aside from that love-between-equals thing (equally messed-up), the movie takes the notion of carefree spirits to the lower depths; it's like an "I Love Lucy" episode done as a junkie melodrama.

### "Around the World in Eighty Days" (1956)

Perfect for the travelers of the zodiac, Mike Todd's globe-hopping, cameo-glutted Oscar-winner (Best Picture) is, in many ways, just a glorified travelogue. But what a travelogue it is. David Niven stars as Phileas Fogg, the nineteenth-century British gentleman who bets his friends that he can, indeed, leave London by hot-air balloon and return (by any means necessary) within the required eighty days. Cantinflas and Shirley MacLaine (as an Indian princess!) are his traveling companions. En route, thanks to Todd's famous-name-dropping strategy, they run into everyone from Bea Lillie and Buster Keaton to Marlene Dietrich and Frank Sinatra. Niven is in almost every scene, and, though he himself was a Pisces (March 1), his Fogg is every bit the unflappable Sag — someone who could make his way around the world with only a top hat and an umbrella.

# SIX TALENTED SAGITTARIANS

**Bette Midler** (December 1, 1945)
With typical Sagittarian extravagance and brashness, she dubbed herself "The Divine Miss M" back when she was still performing in gay bath houses. She was right on the money. While her movie career has had more
ups and downs than you'd expect from someone blessed by Jupiter, the essential Midler has never wavered. She's an amazing triple-threat talent as singer, actress and comic. She also, as her sign suggests, has a high-spirited boldness and a mouth that won't stop. It's that Sag candidness. Why shut up when you can tell the whole truth and nothing but? And tell it in a way that's so outrageously honest and amusing that you get away with it. The epitome of the brassy broad with the big heart, she spoke out on gay rights and AIDS long before it became celebrity-acceptable. Whether her career is in high gear or low, her talent is always divine.

**Suggested rental:** "Big Business" (1988)
Nonstop funny business. Midler and Lily Tomlin play two sets of twins separated at birth and mismatched with each other. One pair grows up in Manhattan where Midler is a monstrous, employee-eating CEO and Tomlin a distracted, fish-out-of-water waif. The other set grows up in the country where Tomlin is a fiestier (and funnier) Norma Rae and Midler is a princess-out-of-water who dreams of credit cards and taxi-cabs. The story is as old as Plautus (the master Roman farceur), but director Jim Abrahams gives it an engagingly fresh spin. So do the stars whose dual roles allow them to double our pleasure and double their fun. The Sag hook? All that unabashed good humor and sunny sense that things will turn out okay even when they don't make a lick of sense. Plus characters who speak their minds . . . double time.

**Sagittarian Moment:** In one scene, the country-fried Bette has to milk a cow, and when it came time to shoot the sequence, she was convinced the animal was going to either kick her or kick over the milk pail ("I can see it in her eye," she insisted). Sure enough, the pail went flying. Midler's comeback: "Well, I guess there's no use crying over spilt milk." What else would a Sag say?

## Woody Allen (December 1, 1935)

You might think that Woody's woebegone persona and fatalistic musings about the human condition are a little too weighty for a supposedly carefree Sagitarian. But remember his earlier, funnier movies like "Bananas," "Sleeper," and "Take the Money and Run"? Even the older, more thoughtful Woody exhibits a version of Sag's essential optimism, as well as Sag's well-known philosophical bent. If Allen has been somewhat careless in his personal life of late, he's always been exacting to a fault in his work. And that innate need for freedom? How about living across Central Park from Mia Farrow and the brood for years. Plus, he's made the movies he wants, the way he wants them, without big-studio interference. That's freedom. And luck. And talent. No wonder Francis Ford Coppola has said he wanted a career like Woody's. Who wouldn't?

**Suggested Rental:** "Annie Hall" (1977)

It's the movie that took away Woody Allen's cult status. At the same time, it started a long-overdue Diane Keaton cult. The plot is as simple as it gets: boy meets girl; boy gets girl; boy loses girl. But it's done as only Woody can, with a series of razor-sharp one-liners and neurotic/acute observations about urban life, love and the pursuit of something approximating happiness in late '70s America. Much like his earlier sketch movies, "Annie Hall" goes all over the place, jumping from past to present, between fantasy and reality, and, in one of the most famous scenes, when Alvy Singer (Allen) and Annie (Keaton) first meet, supplying a running dialogue of what they're really thinking while they make nice-to-meetcha chit-chat. She won a Best Actress Oscar, he won Best Picture and a good time was had by all. Especially the audience.

**Sagittarian Moment:** The entire movie is kind of one big Sag moment, from its humorously philosophical romantic outlook to its life-goes-on acceptance of romantic failure. However, the quintessentially Sag moment comes comes from Alvy's monologue about the guy who tells a shrink that his crazy brother thinks he's a chicken. The shrink asks why doesn't he commit his brother, and the guy says, "I would, but I need the eggs." "That's pretty much how I feel about relationships," Woody/Alvy says. "They're totally irrational and crazy and absurd, but we keep going through it because most of us need the eggs."

## Walt Disney (December 5, 1890)

To a generation of baby boomers, he was Uncle Walt, avuncular host of a series of weekly TV shows that understood (and exploited) product placement and merchandise tie-ins decades before the rest of Hollywood caught on. But he was also one of the most successful, imaginative and influential figures in the history of movies, creating everything from the "Mouse That Roared" to the "Theme Park That Ate the World." Disney's Sagittarian side surfaces in his restless mental energy — he was always looking for new ways to branch out, new things to add to his Magic Kingdom. It's also evident in his self-appointed role as surrogate parent to the nation's children (Sagittarius' teacher/philosopher bent). As his many biographers have pointed out, Disney had his dark side, but in public, in his prime, all kids saw was the magic.

**Suggested Rental:** "Fantasia" (1940)

Disney's folly is a marvel in spite of itself. An attempt to mix Mickey Mouse and Leopold Stokowski, (a typically Sagittarian notion: instruct through entertainment), the movie has dancing hippos, demure centaurs, whirling mushrooms, and a night on Bald Mountain you're not likely to forget (Bela Lugosi was the model for the monster on the mountain top). Considered a flop when it was first released, the movie has since become a classic, partly due to the second chance it received when it was embraced by college-age boomers in the psychedelic '60s who found the movie particularly enjoyable in an, um, altered state. When Art Babbitt, the Disney animator responsible for the mushrooms, was asked if the sequence was drug induced, he reportedly replied, "Yes, it is true. I myself was addicted to Ex-Lax and Feenamint." Groovy!

**Sagittarian Moment:** While it may be true that Disney gushed, "Gee, this'll make Beethoven," after seeing one sequence, the real reason he initiated "Fantasia" was to help his beloved Mickey Mouse's sagging career. He came up with the idea to star Mickey in "The Sorceror's Apprentice," and that became the germ for a feature-length film. Technically speaking, according to the Disney official lore, Mickey is a Scorpio (November 18), but Disney's alter-ego/good-luck charm has always seemed more of a Sag: energetic, optimistic, good-humored and a bit careless (remember what happens in "Sorceror's Apprentice" when those brooms get out of hand?).

# Brad Pitt (December 18, 1963)

For the moment, he is one of our reigning Golden Boys, our designated Male Beauty, our Adonis in blue jeans. He first grabbed our attention (and teenage girls' libidos) as the sexy, insouciant hitchhiker in "Thelma and Louise." Since then, he's been a soulful and perennially depressed undead in "Interview With the Vampire," a cocky Irish terrorist in "The Devil's Own," a magnificently maned heartthrob in "Legends of the Fall" (check his Sag-like entrance on horseback) and an arrogant Aryan mountain climber who discovers his inner spiritual child (the explorer-as-philosopher is very Sag) in "Seven Years in Tibet." His meteoric career may be a manifestation of Sagitarian's "born lucky" streak, but there's definitely more to it than that. After all, great-looking blondes are a dime a two-dozen in Hollywood.

**Suggested Rental:** "A River Runs Through It" (1992)
Reverently directed by Robert Redford from Norman MacLean's acclaimed novella, this lyrical family memoir courses across the screen with the serene sparkle and refreshing purity of an unspoiled mountain stream. Set in rural Montana's Big Sky country between 1910 and 1935, the film focuses on two very different brothers, who were both taught the gospel of fly fishing by their father (Tom Skerritt), a flinty Presbyterian minister. Craig Sheffer is the responsible, straight-arrow older brother. Pitt, as the younger son, isan irresistible wastrel who has an artist's touch with a fly rod. With his tousled hair and golden-boy grin, he's the embodiment of Byronesque youth and beauty — or the young Robert Redford. It's a gloriously filmed, lovingly put-together testamonial to the ties that bind — father to son, brother to brother, lure to line.

**Sagittarian Moment:** The film's celebration of nature and the great outdoors is certainly a draw for Sagittarians. But while Pitt is a natural athlete, he had never done any fly fishing. Before leaving for Montana, he spent weeks practicing his casting from the top of a Hollywood building. Later, in an interview, Pitt said, "I'd hook myself in the back of my head all the time. One time, they had to dig the barb out with pliers." Ah, the joys of method acting.

## Steven Spielberg (December 18, 1947)

How is Steven Spielberg a Sagittarius? Let us count the ways. He is the most successful filmmaker in the world, possibly in history (Jupiter's good fortune). He's made movies about everything from sharks ("Jaws") and dinosaurs ("Jurassic Park") to the Holocaust ("Schindler's List") and slavery ("Amistad") and done them all equally well (versatility). Even his "heaviest" movies emphasize the potential for good in mankind (optimism). Even his "lightest" movies strive for some kind of lesson or moral outlook (the teacher/philosopher). Most of all, like most Sagittarians, he is a master entertainer. Best of all, like most Sagittarians, despite his enormous success, Spielberg has managed to stay connected to his kid side. Never forget, this isn't just Spielberg, the great and powerful; this is also E.T.'s best pal, the kind of guy who'd peddle a bicycle to the moon for you.

**Suggested Rental:** "Raiders of the Lost Ark" (1981)
"E.T." may be closer to Spielberg's heart, but "Raiders of the Lost Ark" is a better example of his Sagittarian love of adventure and fondness for swashbuckling heroes with a deadpan wisecrack for every predicament. Taking their inspiration from old serials like "Flash Gordon," Spielberg and his friend, George Lucas, concocted a triumph of close-calls moviemaking that hurtles from one cliffhanger to the next on the back of a resourceful and engaging hero. Harrison Ford solidified his Han Solo success playing Indiana Jones, an adventurous archeologist caught in a life-and-death race against the Nazis to find a sacred relic. He and Karen Allen (an old flame with some new tricks) are just what the doctor — Doc Savage, that is — ordered. Quite simply, "Raiders" is the most fun to hit the screen since movies came in chapters.

**Sagittarian Moment:** That Sag good luck played a part in the making of "Raiders" at almost every turn. For instance,

Spielberg originally wanted Tom Selleck, but he was tied up with "Magnum P.I." so Ford got the role. While they were shooting, Spielberg got to meet Ford's girlfriend (and later wife), Melissa Mathison, who ended up writing "E.T." Finally, one of the most famous moments in the movie — where Indy tosses his bullwhip aside and shoots the menacing guy with the scimitar — was sheer luck. Ford, who was suffering from dysentery, realized he could save himself a lot of time, trouble and retakes if he just pulled a gun.

## Jane Fonda (December 21, 1937)

Jane Fonda is, was and probably always will be a Sagittarian handful. Whether as Hanoi Jane or as Mrs. Ted Turner, she's always been fearless about speaking her mind, no matter what the cost, personally or professionally. Ironically, her Sagittarian versatility has been more noticeable in her life than in her roles. Or, perhaps more accurately, in the men in her life from whom she's taken her cues as to which Jane she should be. There was Roger Vadim's sex kitten ("Barbarella"), Henry Fonda's devoted but estranged daughter ("On Golden Pond"), Tom Hayden's activist ("The China Syndrome" and "Coming Home"), and, as Mrs. Ted, retirement from films altogether. What often gets lost in all the publicity is the hard-working actress who's won two Oscars. Candid and impulsive (very Sag), she's taken her chances, and she's also taken responsibility for the consequences.

**Suggested Rental:** "Klute" (1971)
As Bree Daniels, the hard-bitten New York prostitute who becomes the NYPD's best clue in an out-of-towner's mysterious disappearance, Fonda won a richly deserved Oscar. Donald Sutherland plays the title role — an investigator tracking the psychopath who may make Bree his next target — but the film's real focus is Fonda. She is strikingly good

as a would-be independent woman who finds herself becoming dependant — emotionally as well as physically — on Sutherland as the killer closes in. In many ways, she is the carefree, don't-tie-me-down Sag being forced by circumstances beyond her control to connect with and trust someone else. A welcome change from Hollywood's patented whore-with-a-heart-of-gold, Bree is a remarkably original creation: bright and sardonic, with nerves of steel when she's plying her trade and a little-girl-lost neuroticism when she's not.

**Sagittarian Moment:** Actually, you could call it an anti-Sagittarian Moment. It came long after shooting was over and the movie was nominated for several Oscars. Fonda was at the height of her activism phase and many wondered what she would say if she won (when she won the Golden Globe the month before, she sent an antiwar Vietnam vet to accept for her). When her name was announced for the Oscar, she came to the podium and said calmly, "There's a lot I could say tonight. But this isn't the time or the place. So I'll just say 'Thank you.'" For once, the Sagittarian held her tongue.

## MOVIES "BORN" AS SAGITTARIANS

| | |
|---|---|
| GONE WITH THE WIND | NIXON |
| HENRY V | JERRY MAGUIRE |
| EDWARD SCISSORHANDS | MARS ATTACKS |
| BUGSY | THE CRUCIBLE |
| THE PRINCE OF TIDES | ALIEN RESURRECTION |
| FRIED GREEN TOMATOES | AMISTAD |
| ALADDIN | TITANIC |
| A FEW GOOD MEN | SPEECHLESS |
| THE PELICAN BRIEF | MRS. DOUBTFIRE |
| DUMB AND DUMBER | SCHINDLER'S LIST |

# OTHER FAMOUS SAGITTARIANS

**NOVEMBER 22**
Jamie Lee Curtis (1958)
Tom Conti (1941)
Terry Gilliam (1940)
Robert Vaughn (1932)
Peter Hall (1930)
Geraldine Page (1924)
Robert M. Young (1924)
Arthur Hiller (1923)
Rodney Dangerfield (1922)
Hoagy Carmichael (1899)

**NOVEMBER 23**
Susan Anspach (1939)
Robert Towne (1934)
Michael Gough (1917)
Victor Jory (1902)
Harpo Marx (1888)
Boris Karloff (1887)

**NOVEMBER 24**
Billy Connolly (1942)
Emir Kosturica (1955)
Howard Duff (1917)
Geraldine Fitzgerald (1913)
Garson Kanin (1912)

**NOVEMBER 25**
Christina Applegate (1971)
Jonathan Kaplan (1947)
Jeffrey Hunter (1926)
Ricardo Montalban (1920)
Jessie Royce Landis (1904)

**NOVEMBER 26**
Tandy Cronyn (1942)
Tina Turner (1938)
Robert Goulet (1933)
Daniel Petrie (1920)
Cyril Cusack (1910)
Frances Dee (1907)

**NOVEMBER 27**
Robin Givens (1964)
Fisher Stevens (1963)
Jimi Hendrix (1942)
Bruce Lee (1940)
Les Blank (1935)
James Agee (1909)

**NOVEMBER 28**
Judd Nelson (1959)
Ed Harris (1950)
Agnieszka Holland (1948)
Joe Dante (1946)
Michael Ritchie (1938)
Hope Lange (1933)
Gloria Grahame (1923)
Lila Skala (1896)

**NOVEMBER 29**
Don Cheadle (1964)
Andrew McCarthy (1962)
Cathy Moriarty (1960)
Jeff Fahey (1956)
Joel Coen (1954)
Howie Mandel (1955)
Diane Ladd (1932)

Busby Berkely (1895)
Yakima Canutt (1895)

*Ben Stiller*

## NOVEMBER 30
Ben Stiller (1965)
Mandy Patinkin (1952)
David Mamet (1947)
Terrence Malick (1943)
Robert Guillaume (1937)
Ridley Scott (1937)
Richard Crenna (1927)
Efrem Zimbalist Jr. (1923)
Virginia Mayo (1920)
Gordon Parks (1912)

*Richard Pryor*

## DECEMBER 1
Treat Williams (1951)
Bette Midler (1945)
Richard Pryor (1940)
Woody Allen (1935)
Dick Shawn (1929)
Eric Rohmer (1920)

Mary Martin (1913)
Gilbert Roland (1905)

## DECEMBER 2
Steven Bauer (1956)
Dennis Christopher (1955)
Julie Harris (1925)
Ray Walston (1914)

## DECEMBER 3
Anna Chlumsky (1981)
Brendan Fraser (1968)
Julianne Moore (1961)
Daryl Hannah (1960)
Hart Bochner (1956)
Diane Kurys (1948)
Jean-Luc Godard (1930)
Sven Nykvist (1922)

*Marisa Tomei*

## DECEMBER 4
Marisa Tomei (1964)
Jeff Bridges (1949)
Horst Buchholz (1933)
Mark Robson (1915)
Buck Jones (1889)

## DECEMBER 5
Jeroen Krabbe (1944)
Otto Preminger (1906)

Emeric Pressburger (1902)
Walt Disney (1901)
Fritz Lang (1890)

## DECEMBER 6
Tom Hulce (1953)
Jobeth Williams (1948)
James Naughton (1945)
Wally Cox (1924)
Agnes Moorehead (1906)
William S. Hart (1865)

## DECEMBER 7
C. THomas Howell (1966)
Ellen Burstyn (1932)
Eli Wallach (1915)
Rod Cameron (1912)
Fay Bainter (1892)

*Kim Basinger*

## DECEMBER 8
Teri Hatcher (1964)
Kim Basinger (1953)
Rick Baker (1950)
Mary Woronov (1943)
James MacArthur (1937)
David Carradine (1936)
Maximilian Schell (1930)
Sammy Davis Jr. (1925)
Lee J. Cobb (1911)

Frank Faylen (1909)
John Qualen (1899)
Georges Melies (1861)

## DECEMBER 9
John Malkovich (1953)
Beau Bridges (1941)
Judi Dench (1934)
Buck Henry (1930)
John Cassavetes (1929)
Dick Van Patten (1928)
Dina Merrill (1925)
Kirk Douglas (1916)
Broderick Crawford (1911)
Doublas Fairbanks Jr. (1909)
Dalton Trumbo (1905)
Margaret Hamilton (1902)
Hermione Gingold (1897)

## DECEMBER 10
Kenneth Branagh (1960)
Tommy Rettig (1941)
Tim Considine (1941)
Tommy Kirk (1941)
Mako (1933)
Dorothy Lamour (1914)
Una Merkel (1903)
Ray Collins (1889)

## DECEMBER 11
Bess Armstrong (1953)
Susan Seidelman (1952)
Teri Garr (1944)
Rita Moreno (1931)
Jean-Louis Trintignant (1930)
Kenneth MacMillan (1929)

Marie Windsor (1924)
Jean Marais (1913)
Carlo Ponti (1912)
Victor McLaglen (1883)

**DECEMBER 12**
Jennifer Connelly (1970)
Wings Hauser (1948)
Frank Sinatra (1915)
Howard Koch (1901)
Edward G. Robinson (1893)
Laura Hope Crews (1879)

**DECEMBER 13**
Steve Buscemi (1957)
Arturo Ripstein (1943)
Richard Zanuck (1934)
Robert Prosky (1930)
Christopher Plummer (1927)
Dick Van Dyke (1925)
Mark Stevens (1916)
Larry Parks (1914)
Curt Jurgens (1912)
Van Heflin (1910)

**DECEMBER 14**
Dee Wallace (1948)
Jane Birkin (1946)
Patty Duke (1946)
Lee Remick (1935)
Abbie Lane (1932)
Deanna Durbin (1921)
Dan Dailey (1913)

**DECEMBER 15**
Helen Slater (1963)

Alex Cox (1954)
Don Johnson (1949)
Tim Conway (1933)
Jeff Chandler (1918)

**DECEMBER 16**
Sam Robards (1961)
Ben Cross (1947)
Liv Ullmann (1939)
Noel Coward (1899)

**DECEMBER 17**
Bill Pullman (1953)
Wes Studi (1947)
Eugene Levy (1946)
Ernie Hudson (1945)
Armin Mueller-Stahl (1920)

**DECEMBER 18**
Brad Pitt (1963)
Ray Liotta (1955)
Gillian Armstrong (1950)
Steven Spielberg (1947)
Alan Rudolph (1943)
Ossie Davis (1917)
Betty Grable (1916)
Jules Dassin (1911)
George Stevens (1904)
Gladys Cooper (1888)
Raimu (1883)

**DECEMBER 19**
Milla Jovovich (1975)
Amy Locane (1972)
Kristy Swanson (1969)
Jennifer Beals (1963)

Cicely Tyson (1933)
Edmund Purdom (1924)
Gordon Jackson (1923)
Ralph Richardson (1902)

**DECEMBER 20**
Jenny Agutter (1952)
George Roy Hill (1922)
Albert Dekker (1905)
Irene Dunne (1898)
Charley Grapewin (1869)

**DECEMBER 21**
Julie Delpy (1969)
Kiefer Sutherland (1966)
Samuel L. Jackson (1948)
Josh Mostel (1946)
Jane Fonda (1937)

# CAPRICORN

## DECEMBER 22 — JANUARY 19

Capricorns don't fool around so, at first glance, the movie biz might seem too frivolous for their determined, ultra-responsible approach to life. Yet it is precisely that slow-but-steady persistence that makes them able to beat the odds in a notoriously unstable profession. Capricorns are in it for the long haul, and they are not deterred by the constant setbacks that are a given in a movie career.

A Capricorn's steely ambition and love of material things rival that of a Leo's, but without the Lion's attention-grabbing flamboyance. Capricorns don't just like power; they live for it. In fact, they won't give up until they get it, and once they have it, they like to keep it. Thus, some of our most enduring stars are Capricorns, such as Cary Grant, Marlene Dietrich, Ava Gardner, Anthony Hopkins, Maggie Smith, and Gerard Depardieu. Capricorns are not usually drawn to comedy but there are exceptions, like Jim Carrey, Diane Keaton, Oliver Hardy and Danny Kaye.

The Capricorn director is as prolific as he is proficient. A prime example is Michael Curtiz, who directed films such as "Casablanca" and "White Christmas" during his fifty-year career. Other notable Capricorns behind the camera include Ismail Merchant, Taylor Hackford, Nicholas Meyer, Fred Schepisi, Sergio Leone, Carol Reed and John Boorman.

And remember, Elvis is a Capricorn. Talk about endurance from beyond the grave . . .

The Capricorn movie-lover is naturally drawn to pictures about successful people – not the prima donnas who attract Leo, but strong-willed achievers with a hardy streak of ruthlessness (just a streak; the real poisoners belong to Scorpio). Given their bent for tradition and order, military films and westerns sit well with Capricorns. So do period pieces, with their innate adherence to a rigid class structure. Movies set in high school appeal for the same pecking-order reasons. Capricorns should probably avoid subversive filmmakers like David Lynch or David Cronenberg. And social satires that challenge the establishment – say, the works of Stanley Kubrick or Preston Sturges – aren't best bets.

## FIVE SUGGESTED RENTALS

**"Alien"** (1979)
What it lacks in humanity, Ridley Scott's terrific haunted-house-in-space thriller more than makes up for in monster. And monster is what this terrifyingly effective film is all about. A creature as horrifying and hungry as Bruce the Shark, and as ooey-gooey messy as little Linda Blair full of pea soup, is loose on a space ship. Tom Skerritt, John Hurt, Harry Dean Stanton and Yaphet Kotto are among the unfortunate crew who get downsized – quite literally – one by one. But the star of the show is Sigourney Weaver, whose

won't-give-an-inch battle with the Alien represents Capricorn self-reliance and determination in circumstances that go beyond the extreme. And, like so many Capricorns, she initially commands our respect rather than our affection. It would take the "Alien" sequels (there are three more in the series) to give us time to find the woman within the warrior.

**"The Untouchables"** (1987)
Gangbusters — just like its fearless G-men heroes. Director Brian De Palma finally found a genre that suited him — tabloid opera. As punchy as a headline and as pretentious as a diva's aria, this is a brutal beauty of a movie set in a '30s Chicago full of machine gun battles and bootleg gin. Unlike Robert Stack in the '60s TV series, this Ness (Kevin Costner) is young and untried — a straight-arrow underdog who, with the help of the last honest cop in Chicago (Sean Connery), undergoes a baptism by gunfire and is himself somewhat corrupted in the process. Connery, who won an Oscar, and Robert De Niro (as Al Capone, evil incarnate), provide the flash, but Costner holds the movie together with graceful Capricorn-like diligence and law-and-order rigidity. Don't look for subtleties; just enjoy it for what it is — a mobster morality play done in bold, rat-a-tat style.

**"The Great Santini"** (1979)
Based on Pat Conroy's semiautobiographical novel, this family drama packs one hell of an emotional punch. Set in the early '60s in the small, bucolic town of Beaufort, South Carolina, the film is about growing up in the combat zone that passed as a home life for the Meechum family, under the spit-and-polish tyranny of Col. Bull Meechum (Capricorn Robert Duvall), the self-dubbed "Great Santini." Blythe Danner, as the star's supportive, long-suffering wife, and Michael O'Keefe, as the sensitive son who learns how to love his father, give remarkable performances. But the film's centerpiece is Duvall. A warrior without a war, he shows us the

dark side of Capricorn's iron-willed ambition and emotional remoteness. Selfish and inflexible - as Capricorns can be - he is a magnificent monster, as much at war with himself as with those he loves.

### "Marlene" (1984)

Sort of a self-portrait of a Capricorn as a conundrum. Juxtaposing myth and mortality, actor-turned-director Maximilian Schell created a unique documentary about Marlene Dietrich, his one-time co-star in "Judgement at Nuremberg." When the legendary Dietrich refused to appear on-camera during their interviews, Schell was forced to improvise. The result is a fascinating blend of fact (his) and fantasy (hers). We overhear Dietrich's unmistakable husky, blase baritone as we see clips, newsreels and shots of Schell trying to figure out how to make a film about someone who won't allow herself to be filmed. He has called it "a film of denial," and sometimes the denials are hilarious (when Dietrich says she's an only child, Schell shows us a photo of herself and her sister). The work is part tribute, part sparring match and totally intriguing. Marlene Dietrich knows what becomes a legend best. Not mink, but mystery.

### "The Wings of the Dove" (1997)

This subtle and seductive version of Henry James's novel looks like a Merchant-Ivory film and sounds like a Merchant-Ivory film, but its dark, conflicted heart is worthy of a film noir. Helena Bonham Carter stars as the very Capricorn heroine — a woman who, forbidden by her own adherence to the rules and snobberies of Edwardian England, cannot marry her lover (Linus Roache), a penniless journalist. When she finds that her new best friend, an orphaned heiress (Alison Elliott), not only has taken a shine to Roache but is also dying, she orchestrates a dangerous love affair. Her emotional ruthlessness is an utterly Capricorn approach to a seemingly insoluble state of affairs. The movie's strength is in its performances and the way it remains tantalizingly non-commital about Bonham Carter's true motives. A whisper-smart picture about strong-willed manipulation gone awry.

## SIX FAMOUS CAPRICORNS

### Kevin Costner (January 18, 1955)

Sometimes, it's hard to be the hero. But in movies, somebody's got to do it, and Costner's been doing it about as well as it can be done since the mid-'80s. He's played everyone from Elliott Ness to Robin Hood to Wyatt Earp and he's played them as only a Capricorn could or would — as straightforward, straight-arrows with only a hint of the boyish rebelliousness he charmed us with in "Bull Durham," "Silverado" and "Field of Dreams." Whether standing up for God, country or Whitney Houston, he's shown an unshakable integrity and inner strength that's sometimes been scoffed at as old-fashioned and "unhip" (remember when Madonna had him for lunch in "Truth or Dare?"). Sure, Costner could learn to lighten up a bit and not take himself so seriously. But then, he probably wouldn't be Costner, and he certainly wouldn't be a Capricorn.

**Sugggested Rental:** "Wyatt Earp" (1994)
Directed by fellow Capricorn, Lawrence Kasdan, this very good western is a good half-hour too long. But that's because the film insists on telling us the whole story, following the famed lawman from his Kansas boyhood to his adventures out West, as he ricochets from Wichita to Dodge and finally, to Tombstone and thirty seconds of immortality at the OK Corral. Dennis Quaid is superb as the consumptive killer, Doc Holliday, who becomes Wyatt's unlikely friend. Capricorns will like the movie's epic deliberateness and its workmanlike refusal to glamorize characters or events. Kasdan and Costner clearly

love the myth of the West, but they respect its reality, too. As Wyatt says, "Sometimes even I don't know what really happened. But I do know this. The stories are always better."

**Capricorn Moment:** Kasdan, who first discovered Costner in "The Big Chill" and then famously cut him from the movie, said what he saw in the actor was "the quintessential American man. . . . He believes in all the things that are the best hope for this country – loyalty, steadfastness, strength. . . . He's also stubborn and inflexible, like all Americans." Or did he mean, "like all Capricorns"?

## Faye Dunaway (January 14, 1941)

Everything about her is high-powered and glossy – from her enviable cheekbones to the diva temperament. Whether robbing banks in "Bonnie and Clyde" or raging about wire hangers in "Mommie, Dearest," Dunaway has always commanded our attention, respect and, maybe, just a tinge of fear. This a woman to be reckoned with – as Jack Nicholson and Steve McQueen learned in "Chinatown" and "The Thomas Crowne Affair" respectively. If she were a man, Dunaway would've probably been cast in traditional Capricorn-ish, stand-tall hero roles. As a woman, she's been asked to play schemers or shrews. Still, even her cruelest parts have showcased her keen intelligence and unmistakable presence. A woman whose every move seems like a grand entrance, she may be a bit flashy for Capricorns, but then, most of them love those hard, shiny surfaces.

**Suggested Rental:** "Network" (1976)

This multiple Oscar-winner's predictions of whither TV looked positively outrageous in the mid-'70s. Now they look like yesterday's news. Literally. Paddy Chayesvsky's jocularly lurid vision of television news as packaging, not content, has become all too true all too quickly. Peter Finch won a posthumous Best Actor Oscar for his "mad as hell" (and mad as a hatter) anchorman. Dunaway matched him every step of the way (including receiving a Best Actress Oscar) as the manipulative and glamorous network exec who knows all too well that the future of news is in entertainment, not the truth. With her smooth ruthlessness, her canny power plays and her unrepentant careerism, she's Capricorn the hard way- selfish, materialistic and unstoppable. Not necessarily a pret- ty picture, but pretty darn fascinating. And good, bilious fun.

**Capricon Moment:** Dunaway's character must seduce anoth- er network exec, played by William Holden, in her inexorable rise to the top. At their first dinner together, she tries the "vulnerable" approach by reciting a litany of her failed rela- tionships. "It seems I'm inept at everything," she sighs win- ningly. "Except my work. So I confine myself to that. All I want out of life is a thirty share and a twenty rating." Spoken like a true workaholic Capricorn.

## Cary Grant (January 18, 1904)

Had enough of hearing how cold and careerist Capricorns can be? How about find- ing out that the most charming man in movies was a Capricorn? True, it's said that Cary Grant was nothing like his on-screen persona. Rather, in real life, he was cool and careerist. But what a cover! The legend goes that Mae West saw him on the studio lot in 1933 and said, "If he can talk, I'll take him." He could and she did. We all did. For thirty-five years and sev- enty-two movies, we couldn't get enough of Cary Grant: His airy elusiveness, the mischief-tinged mystery, the delicious destraction balanced by baleful stares or the self-possessed watchfulness under the silly buoyancy. But as Archibald Leach (his real name) often reminded us, "Cary Grant" was a consciously created dream-self: "1 pretended to be a certain kind of man on screen, and 1 became that man in life. 1 became me." Good work, Archie.

**Suggested Rental:** "The Philadelphia Story" (1941)
Mainlining it with Grant, Katharine Hepburn, Jimmy Stewart and director George Cukor. Hepburn is Tracy Lord, the imperious Philadelphia aristocrat and irresistible spoiled brat (the Hepburn "type" in the '30s and '40s) whose society wedding is derailed by her ex-husband's (Grant) untimely reappearance and a pair of tabloid reporters (Stewart and Ruth Hussey). The movie pokes fun at the upper crust, but in a friendly, affectionate way that won't threaten tradition-upholding, status-quo loving Capricorns. The picture is clearly a Hepburn vehicle — she played it on stage, bought the rights and parlayed it into her film comeback after being labled "box office poison." However, it's Grant's sparkling, self-mocking performance that gives the movie its slightly tipsy, off-kilter tone. Stewart won the Oscar, but Grant won the day — and the girl.

**Capricorn Moment:** As usual, there was the extreme dichotomy between Grant on screen and off. In the movie, he's the epitome of airy, heedless charm; in real life, he donated his entire salary to the British war effort. Stanley Donen, who later directed Grant in a couple of films, summed up his performance thusly: "He always seemed real . . . but it was the magic that came from enormous amounts of work." Pure Capricorn — working extra hard to make it look effortless.

## Mel Gibson (January 3, 1956)

He was named *People* magazine's "Sexiest Man Alive" in 1985 — a distinction that still makes him wince. Then he won a slew of Oscars for "Braveheart" in 1995 — a distinction that still makes his "just another pretty face" critics wince. Yet Gibson has proven himself to be far more than "just another . . ." When he first hit it big in movies like "Gallipoli" and "The Road Warrior," one New York critic wrote, "I don't know what star quality is, but whatever it is, Gibson's got it." He's also got a Capricorn's stubborn adherence to conservative values which, combined with his Capricorn plain-spokenness, has sometimes gotten him into trouble with the liberal media. Gibson couldn't care less. Even his detractors will admit his rough-hewn, unpredictable appeal is unlike anyone else's working in movies these days. What other "Sexiest Man Alive" has played "Hamlet"?

**Suggested Rental:** "Braveheart" (1995)
At the heart of Gibson's tumultuously entertaining epic is the almost-quaint notion that movie heroics should mean something more than an obvious play for that much-coveted eighteen-to-twenty-five box-office demographic. Gibson's picture extolls such old-fashioned (read, Capricorn-like) virtues as honor, freedom, principle, loyalty and romantic love. The star, who also directed, plays William Wallace, a bonnie thirteenth-century Scotsman who gave the English hell for trying to make hash (not haggis) out of his homeland. A loose adaptation of Wallace's myth-enshrouded exploits, the film runs almost three hours. But with its ferociously brutal battles, romantic trysts, snotty court intrigues (coolly orchestrated by Patrick McGoohan as the evil Edward 1) and squabbling rival clans, you hardly notice. Good for Mel, Scotland and Saint Cinema!

**Capricorn Moment:** While he admitted that getting the "real" story on William Wallace was about as easy as getting the facts on Robin Hood, Gibson took his history as seriously as possible. That included the blue warpaint, the modest Scottish castles (more like wooden forts) and even — he swears — the famous butt-baring scene. But this Capricorn's most dogged dive into Scottish tradition came when he insisted on sampling haggis (oats and sweetbreads in a boiled sheep's tummy). "It's really quite delicious," he gamely claimed. "And the good thing is, it looks the same going in as coming out."

## Denzel Washington (December 28, 1954)

When they remade "The Bishop's Wife" as "The Preacher's Wife," guess who got cast in the role originally played by Cary Grant? Coincidence or . . . in the stars? Like Grant, Washington is a world-class charmer, one of the best-looking, sheerly likable men working in movies these days. And, like Grant, he can balance his romantic-comedy side with straight-on heroes. Grant did it in his Hitchcock collaborations; Washington does it in films like "Glory" (for which he won an Oscar) and "Philadelphia." He's gone mainstream in "The Pelican Brief" and art-house in "Mississippi Masala," and he combined the two in "Malcolm X." And while nobility can almost be a bad word to use about an actor in the '90s, he is noble (fall-out from Capricorn's dedication, most likely). Yet he somehow makes it seem hip. Put bluntly, he humanizes perfection.

**Suggested Rental:** "Courage Under Fire" (1996)

Washington plays a military officer assigned to review the Medal of Honor candidacy of a pilot killed in combat during the Gulf War. The twist? The pilot is a woman (Meg Ryan). Instead of rubber-stamping the case, as his superiors and the media so clearly wish him to, Washington conducts a full and unbiased investigation. In doing so, he uncovers a "Rashomon"-like web of conflicting stories and even a possible cover-up, thus bringing into question his own relationship with the military (a very Capricorn conflict — honoring the truth versus honoring entrenched tradition). A rich and rewarding movie, "Courage Under Fire" has everything from guts-and-glory combat scenes worthy of John Wayne, to post-Watergate paranoia about the nature of truth in an age of photo-ops. The excellent supporting cast includes a then-unknown Matt Damon, Scott Glenn and Lou Diamond Phillips.

**Capricorn Moment:** Though Ryan's character is central to the plot, the central conflict is Washington's quest to discover his place in the military and in his family (kind of a pre-midlife crisis). Director Ed Zwick says he felt the character's defining moment comes when Washington, having gone off to live on his own, finally returns home and uprights a bike lying in the yard that belongs to one of his kids. The gesture, Zwick insists, signifies the character's willingness to again reassume responsibility — as all Capricorns ultimately must do.

## Jim Carrey (January 17, 1962)

Meet the Capricorn who could easily qualify as the anti-Capricorn. At first glance, Jim Carrey embodies everything Capricorns shun; he's an unpredictable, over-the-top exhibitionist whose fearless foolishness runs the gamut from dumb to dumber to dumbest. But look beyond the limber-limbed pandemonium of the "Ace Ventura" movies and "Dumb and Dumber," and you'll find someone with Capricorn's workaholic dedication and unwavering, one-step-at-a-time determination to make it to the top. Most recent step: the critically acclaimed "The Truman Show." Though he seemed to come out of nowhere (other than being the designated white guy on "In Living Color"), this overnight sensation took fifteen years to arrive (blink twice and you'll miss him in "The Dead Pool" and "Peggy Sue Got Married"). Now that he's here, he's probably going to stay awhile — antic, dangerous and laughing all the way to the bank.

**Suggested Rental:** "The Mask" (1994)
The Looney Tunes spirits of Tex Avery and Chuck Jones hover like prankster guardian angels over this shamelessly silly, determinedly frenetic live-action cartoon. Carrey plays a nerdy bank clerk who stumbles across an ancient mask with transforming powers. He puts it on and becomes an id-driven alter-ego called The Mask, who's ready to take on the world. And, thanks to the wizardry of Industrial Light and Magic, he has the special-effects arsenal to do it. The plot is about as pertinent as the plot of a Hong Kong action flick. Basically, it's just an excuse for Carrey to fold and mutate like the lead 'Toon in a "Roger Rabbit" sequel. Yet he's as sweet as he is manic, and his boy-next-door good looks (kind of a adrenalized mix of Dean Jones, John Davidson and Peter Marshall) make "The Mask" the perfect Jekyll-and-Hyde tale for the morphing generation.

**Capricorn Moment:** Surprisingly, Carrey had no trouble at all relating to The Mask's mild-mannered alter-ego. In Stanley Ipkiss, the milquetoast bank clerk and all-purpose doormat. Carrey says he found "the part of me that can't express myself. He's just the character I wanna play . . . the good man who feels pain but still tries to get above it." Hmm, sounds suspiciously like a Kevin Costner hero.

## MOVIES "BORN" AS CAPRICORNS

| | |
|---|---|
| JESSE JAMES | THE PRINCE OF TIDES |
| ALWAYS | THE HAND THAT ROCKS THE |
| GLORY |   CRADLE |
| DRIVING MISS DAISY | HOFFA |
| KINDERGARTEN COP | LORENZO'S OIL |
| THE BONFIRE OF THE | GRUMPY OLD MEN |
|   VANITIES | PHILADELPHIA |
| THE GODFATHER PART III | NELL |
| FRIED GREEN TOMATOES | COBB |

THE PEOPLE VS. LARRY
FLYNT
THE POSTMAN

WAG THE DOG
THE CRYING GAME

## OTHER FAMOUS CAPRICORNS

**DECEMBER 22**
Ralph Fiennes (1962)
Hector Elizondo (1936)
Peggy Ashcroft (1907)

**DECEMBER 23**
Corey Haim (1972)
Harry Shearer (1943)
Elizabeth Hartman (1941)
Peter Medak (1937)
Frederic Forrest (1936)
Harry Guardino (1925)
John Cromwell (1887)

**DECEMBER 24**
Nicholas Meyer (1945)
Jill Bennett (1931)
Ava Gardner (1922)
Howard Hughes (1905)
Michael Curtiz (1888)
Ruth Chatterton (1893).

**DECEMBER 25**
Sissy Spacek (1949)
Hanna Schygulla (1943)
Ismail Merchant (1936)
Rod Serling (1924)
Mike Mazurski (1909)
Cab Calloway (1907)

**DECEMBER 26**
Jared Leto (1971)
John Lynch (1961)
Fred Schepisi (1939)
Donald Moffat (1930)
Alan King (1927)
Richard Widmark (1914)
Elisha Cook Jr. (1903)

**DECEMBER 27**
Gerard Depardieu (1948)
John Amos (1939)
Michel Piccoli (1925)
Marlene Dietrich (1901)
Sydney Greenstreet (1879)

**DECEMBER 28**
Denzel Washington (1954)
Nichelle Nichols (1936)
Maggie Smith (1934)
Martin Milner (1927)

*Sissy Spacek*

Lew Ayres (1908)
F. W. Murnau (1889)

**DECEMBER 29**
Jason Gould (1971)
Jon Polito (1950)
Ted Danson (1947)
Jon Voight (1938)
Viveca Lindfors (1920)
George Marshall (1891)

**DECEMBER 30**
Caroline Goodwyn (1964)
Tracey Ullman (1959)
Sheryl Lee Ralph (1956)
Russ Tamblyn (1934)
Jo Van Fleet (1919)
Carol Reed (1906)

*Anthony Hopkins*

**DECEMBER 31**
Gong Li (1965)
Val Kilmer (1959)
Bebe Neuwirth (1958)
James Remar (1953)
Joe Dellesandro (1948)
Tim Mathison (1947)
Taylor Hackford (1945)
Barbara Carrera (1945)
Bern Kingsley (1943)

Sarah Miles (1941)
Sean S. Cunningham (1941)
Anthony Hopkins (1937)

**JANUARY 1**
Don Novello (1943)
Frank Langella (1940)
Matthew "Stymie" Beard (1925)
Dana Andrews (1912)
Basil Dearden (1911)
Charles Bickford (1889)

**JANUARY 2**
Todd Haynes (1961)
Joanna Pacula (1957)

**JANUARY 3**
Mel Gibson (1956)
Dabney Coleman (1932)
Robert Loggia (1930)
Sergio Leone (1929)
Ray Milland (1907)
Anna May Wong (1905)
Zasu Pitts (1898)
Marion Davies (1897)

**JANUARY 4**
Julia Ormond (1965)
Matt Freur (1958)
Ann Magnusen (1956)
George P. Cosmatos (1941)
Dyan Cannon (1937)
Carlos Saura (1932)
Barbara Rush (1927)
Sterling Holloway (1905)

*Diane Keaton*

## JANUARY 5
Suzy Amis (1958)
Pamela Sue Martin (1953)
Diane Keaton (1946)
Robert Duvall (1937)
George Reeves (1914)
Jean-Pierre Aumont (1909)

## JANUARY 6
John Singleton (1968)
Rowan Atkinson (1955)
Anthony Minghella (1954)
Capucine (1933)
Danny Thomas (1914)
Loretta Young (1913)
Tom Mix (1880)

*Nicolas Cage*

## JANUARY 7
Nicolas Cage (1964)
Vincent Gardenia (1922)
Butterfly mcQueen (1911)
Adolph Zukor (1873)

## JANUARY 8
Gaby Hoffman (1982)
John McTiernan (1951)
David Bowie (1947)
Yvette Mimieux (1942)
Graham Chapman (1941)
Elvis Presley (1935)
Roy Kinnear (1934)
Larry Storch (1925)
Ron Moody (1924)

## JANUARY 9
David Johanson (1950)
Susannah York (1941)
Lee Van Cleef (1925)
Herbert Lom (1917)
Fernando Lamas (1915)
Anita Louise (1915)
Vilma Banky (1898)

## JANUARY 10
Trini Alvarado (1967)
Walter Hill (1942)
Sal Mineo (1939)
Paul Heinreid (1908)
Ray Bolger (1904)
Frances X. Bushman (1883)

## JANUARY 11
Joely Richardson (1965)
Stanley Tucci (1960)
Rod Taylor (1930)
Lionel Stander (1908)
Eva LaGallienne (1899)
George Zucco (1886)

## JANUARY 12
Jeremy Northam (1961)
Kirstie Alley (1955)
Howard Stern (1954)
Wayne Wang (1949)
Luise Rainer (1910)

## JANUARY 13
Patrick Dempsey (1966)
Penelope Ann Miller (1964)
Julia Louis-Dreyfus (1961)
Kevin Anderson (1959)
Gwen Verdon (1925)
Robert Stack (1919)
Kay Francis (1903)

## JANUARY 14
Jason Bateman (1969)
Steven Soderbergh (1963)
Lawrence Kasdan (1949)
Carl Weathers (1948)
Faye Dunaway (1941)
Tom Tryon (1926)
William Bendix (1906)
Hal Roach (1892)

## JANUARY 15
Chad Lowe (1968)
Julian Sands (1958)
Mario Van Peebles (1957)
Andrea Martin (1947)
Margaret O'Brien (1937)
Lloyd Bridges (1913)
Torin Thatcher (1905)
Ernest Thesiger (1879)

## JANUARY 16
Debbie Allen (1950)
John Carpenter (1948)
Richard Bohringer (1941)
Katy Jurado (1924)
Ethel Merman (1909)
Karl Freund (1890)
Lloyd Bacon (1890)

## JANUARY 17
Jim Carrey (1962)
David Caruso (1956)
Kevin Reynolds (1952)
Andy Kaufman (1949)
Sheree North (1933)
James Earl Jones (1931)
Mack Sennett (1880)
Carl Laemmle (1867)

## JANUARY 18
Kevin Costner (1955)
John Boorman (1933)
Constance Moore (1922)
Danny Kaye (1913)
Cary Grant (1904)
Oliver Hardy (1892)

## JANUARY 19
Dolly Parton (1946)
Shelley Fabares (1944)
Michael Crawford (1942)
Tippi Hedren (1935)
Richard Lester (1932)
Fritz Weaver (1926)
Jean Stapleton (1923)
Guy Madison (1922)

# AQUARIUS

## JANUARY 20 — FEBRUARY 18

Aquarius is the only sign ever to have a movie made about it (all together now: "This is the dawning of . . ."). Okay, sorry, that was a low blow.

But "Hair" notwithstanding — a movie that wasn't the dawning of anything, much less anyone's career — those born under the sign of the Water Bearer are not, at first glance, a good Hollywood fit. They are too idealistic, too lacking in vanity, too unconventional, too humanitarian, too . . . well, you get the idea.

That's probably why Aquarians who do make a career in movies stand out for very specific reasons. They can be out-spoken — like Vanessa Redgrave, Alan Alda and Jeanne Moreau. Or rebels — like James Dean, John Belushi and Mia Farrow. Or simply tremendously humane human beings — like François Truffaut, Paul Newman and John Travolta.

The visionary thing comes easily to the nonconformist

Aquarian (think, David Lynch and Federico Fellini). Yet just as strong is their stubborn adherence to being themselves, that is, doing their own thing (think, Humphrey Bogart, Gene Hackman and, in her own nutty way, Carmen Miranda).

Freedom is a key word for Aquarians — freedom for themselves and for others. The Aquarian movie-goer is naturally attracted to films that explore social issues in an activist manner. "Amistad," "Norma Rae" and "A Man for All Seasons" (starring Aquarian Paul Scofield) come to mind. Conversely, they're also drawn to the works of fellow Aquarian and notorious conservative, John Ford. That's because his movies always stress the importance of the individual — another key Aquarian concept. And for Aquarius' goofy side, check out the sci-fi section.

Not recommended: by-the-book comedies (say, anything by a former "Saturday Night Live" regular); formulaic slasher films (seen one killer, seen 'em all); bloated disaster flicks; or lush '50s-style religious epics.

## FIVE SUGGESTED RENTALS

**"Invasion of the Body Snatchers"** (1978)
You certainly can't go wrong with the 1956 original (starring fellow Aquarian Kevin McCarthy), but Aquarians will get a special kick out of Philip Kaufman's remake because of the way it weaves so much "Age of Aquarius" late '70s psychobabble into the story of giant pods from outer space who create soulless clones of human beings. As a reworking of Don Siegel's classic, the movie could've been just a soulless clone itself. Instead, this plant lover's nightmare offers great style, wit and a number of in-jokes (look for appearances by both Siegel and McCarthy). The setting is a do-your-own-thing San Francisco where health inspector Donald Sutherland concludes that giant pods constitute a definite health hazard for himself

and costars Leonard Nimoy and Jeff Goldblum. The ultimate pro-individuality movie for the ultimate pro-individuality sign.

### "The Long Walk Home" (1990)

This beautifully observed, emotionally acute drama about the 1955 Montgomery bus boycott shows us the first halting steps in a journey that still isn't finished. Sissy Spacek and Whoopi Goldberg costar as a Southern housewife (the Junior League sort) and maid (the full-time sort) who are both irrevocably changed by the boycott first sparked by Rosa Parks' historic "Just Say No" (she refused to give up her bus seat to a white guy, as was required by law). The plain 'n' simple plot is the stuff TV movies are made of and there is a whiff of white-glove do-gooding in the restrained, understated tone. But director Richard Pearce and his superb cast take us past a knee-jerk response by putting two human faces on change by celebrating small acts of courage. As hard to shake as a childhood memory, this movie will give Aquarius' social conscience its money's worth.

### "Phenomenon" (1996)

This flick is as phenomenally likable as its star, Aquarian John Travolta. He plays a nice-guy, small-town mechanic with a dog, a garden, some good friends (farmer Forrest Whitaker, town doc Robert Duvall) and a serious crush on single mom, Kyra Sedgwick. His life is up-ended when a mysterious light (a literal bolt from the blue) transforms him into a genius with telekinetic and psychic powers. Though it starts out as a harmless, warm-hearted fantasy, the movie deepens into something more thoughtful and complex. Aquarians will respond to its open-minded embrace of other-wordly aspects in everyday events and its life-affirming spirit. But Travolta's performance is the picture's lynchpin. He's radiantly charming as the bumpkin-turned Einstein — thrilled by his new intellectual curiosity and his surprise awakening to the miraculous interconnectedness of all living things.

### "Liquid Sky" (1982)

A movie that's cheerfully out of its mind, assuming it has a mind. Directed by a Russian èmigrè named Slava Tsukerman, who moved to New York and, as far as anyone knows, never made another film, "Liquid Sky" is a heady mixture of sex, drugs, rock 'n' roll and extraterrestrials. A teensy space ship lands in Manhattan, and its inhabitants are looking for a high they get from heroin or, better yet, from human sexual pleasure. They zero in on Margaret (Anne Carlisle), a rainbow-faced, malaise-ridden, mannequin-like fashion model who's unwittingly turned into a real femme fatale. That is, make it with Margaret and you're a goner. Part "War of the Worlds," part Andy Warhol, the movie doesn't give a Day-Glo damn about making sense, but in its own punked-out way, it's quite funny and unconventional enough for the most unconventional Aquarian.

### "Dead Man" (1996)

The Wild West becomes the Weird West in Jim Jarmusch's mytho-poetic meditation on a beloved genre. A mild-mannered accountant (Johnny Depp) goes west for a job that no longer exists. He finds himself branded an outlaw and embarks on a very Aquarian odyssey that takes him from so-called civilization to a natural state that's both savage and enlightened. His traveling companion/spiritual guide is a jumbo-sized Native American, played with laconic jocularity by Gary Farmer. Depp's charismatic impassivity as the accountant-turned-killer serves Jarmusch's purposes well. The pace is maddeningly slow, and the allegory can be heavy-handed (hey, it's Jarmusch), but the film's hipster whimsy and elliptical narrative are a piece of cake for intuitive risk-takers like Aquarius. Look for Robert Mitchum, John Hurt, Gabriel Byrne and Crispin Glover in tiny roles.

## SIX FAMOUS AQUARIANS

**James Dean** (February 8, 1931)

He lived fast, died young and left a beautiful corpse. Plus a legend that continues to grow over a quarter of a century after his death in an automobile accident at age twenty-four. Dean only made three movies — "Giant," "Rebel Without a Cause" and "East of Eden" — but in them he established an iconic figure that spoke directly to (and for) the restless, alienated '50s teens who didn't identify with Sandra Dee and Troy Donahue. His brooding good looks and neurotic intensity gave him the aura of a betrayed romantic — the Aquarian idealist who's been buffeted about by life a few times too many. The enduring beyond-the-grave nature of his celebrity — fans still flock to the cemetery in Fairmount, Indiana, where he's buried — gives the whole Dean phenomenon an eerie, other-worldly twinge. As if, in typical Aquarian fashion, he'd rebelled against death itself.

**Suggested Rental:** "Rebel Without a Cause" (1955)

Being a mixed-up kid never seemed as sexy as it does in Nicholas Ray's tale of a tormented teen (Dean) trying to connect — with the kids at his new high school, with the girl next door (gorgeous Natalie Wood) and with his clueless parents (weakling dad, Jim Backus, and shrewish mom, Ann Doran). The plot really isn't much — a misunderstood adolescent from a typical "good" home can't seem to stay out of trouble (remember the famous "playing chicken" scene?). But Ray and his cast (add Sal Mineo as Dean's hero-worshipping pal) give the soap-opera narrative an added resonance. Like all Aquarians, their characters are truth-seekers and risk-takers, especially Dean, whose performance played chicken with an entire generation's self-image. And the "alternative family" the three stars form presages similar groups that emerged a decade later in the age of you-know-what.

**Aquarian Moment:** "Don't we give you everything you want?" Dean's parents ask him in the movie. They do — materially. But emotionally, he's totally deprived. And material things always matter less to Aquarians than just about anything else. When he finds one of the school bullies has slashed his tires, he simply drawls, "You know something? You read too many comic books."

## Mia Farrow (February 9, 1945)

She's the flower-child waif who captured the hearts (for a while, at least) of power players Frank Sinatra and Woody Allen. A manifestation, perhaps, of Aquarius' tendency to make inappropriate associations? Yet, as the very public and very bitter battle with Allen proved, underneath the soft-focus vulnerability was a prehensile steeliness — an Aquarian as a morally-fired-up activist. Her devotion to her large and culturally-diverse brood of children, both natural and adopted, evince her Aquarian altruism and generosity. Roman Polanski captured her ethereal child-woman allure best in "Rosemary's Baby," but her best acting was in her decade's-worth of work she did with Woody. Hers has been a highly individualistic (read, Aquarian) career. It's difficult to see her going the usual ingenue route and fading into the movie sunset of Hallmark-card moms or addled aunts.

**Suggested Rental:** "A Midsummer Night's Sex Comedy" (1982) Woody Allen goes wistful in a movie that aspires to do nothing more than give us a few smiles for a summer night. And it does. The film is set at the turn of the century over an insanely beautiful weekend in the country where three couples — Allen and Mary Steenburgen, Jose Ferrer and Farrow, Tony Roberts and Julie Hagerty — play mix-and-match romantic games under the stars. Lightly Chekovian in tone, the picture offers lunatic farce and bittersweet sentiment dressed up in boaters and belted waists. Yet it's also as enchanted and fanciful as its Shakespearean namesake. A nice Woody touch: Puck's part is played by aroused libidos and a metallic "spirit ball" that supposedly communes with the dead (it's one of Allen's character's nutty inventions). Cinematographer Gordon Willis streams pure magic through his lens. By day, he out-goldens "On Golden Pond;" by night, the movie seems lit by moonbeams.

**Aquarian Moment:** The movie was not a huge hit when it was first released, possibly because its tone of romantic whimsy and spirits dancing in the woods wasn't exactly what Allen's fans expected. Yet that's precisely what gives it its Aquarian aura. At the end, the Ferrer character, who's scoffed at "spirits and pixies" throughout the picture, reveals that the woods are inhabited by the glowing spirits of those who died while making love. Aquarians will *melt*.

### John Travolta (February 18, 1954)

He was a has-been before he was thirty-five and, by his own calculation, had made no fewer than six comebacks by the time he turned forty. No wonder John Travolta has been labeled The Comeback Kid. Of course, with typical Aquarian progressiveness, he prefers the word "reemergence." In the late '70s, he was the hottest thing going, with back-to-back blockbusters like "Saturday Night Fever" and "Grease." By the late '80s, though, he couldn't get arrested. Then came Travolta's reemergence in "Pulp Fiction," followed by roles in "Get Shorty," "Face/Off" and "Primary Colors." Now that he's back on the A-list, Travolta takes his reversal of fortune with Aquarian tolerance and good nature. He holds no grudges from the past and has no expectations for the future. As he said after "Pulp Fiction," "I'm thrilled at the recognition, but I'll never again think it's going to be that way forever."

**Suggested Rental:** "Michael" (1996)
Sort of an uneven winged victory. The angel Travolta plays in this appealing fantasy-romance isn't the sort for whom little bells tinkle. More slovenly guest than heavenly host, he's a beer-swilling chain-smoker with a two-day stubble and a middle-aged gut. He first appears to an Iowa motel manager (Jean Stapleton), but his true mission is to change the lives of two tabloid reporters (William Hurt and Andie MacDowell) sent to do a story about him by their short-fused boss (Bob Hoskins). The film is gooey as all get-out. But it's good goo, the kind that puts you in a good-will-toward-everyone mood, which is how most true Aquarians function every day, with or without an angel to guide them. And while you don't need to be an Aquarian to appreciate the sight of Vinnie Barbarino and Edith Bunker dancing together in the snowy streets of Chicago, it might help.

**Aquarian Moment:** Reportedly, Travolta wasn't initially all that interested in writer/director Nora Ephron's script. After all, he was being sent just about everything in Hollywood at that time. But Steven Spielberg, of all people, called up and encouraged him to read it. Travolta later said, "I think I must have the best guardian angels on the planet." The perfect Aquarian response — altruistic with a spiritual touch.

**David Lynch** (January 20, 1946)
There's a side to Aquarius that's just, well, for lack of a better word, just a little whacko. And that's the side we get with David Lynch, weirdo provocateur. On the surface, Lynch appears to be as all-American as Mom and  apple pie. Which is, in a sense, quite true if you remember that Mrs. Bates was someone's Mom, too. Lynch seems incapable of making an ordinary film. His best-known works — "Blue Velvet" and the television series, "Twin Peaks" — hit

America right in the middle of its id. Dreamier films like "Eraserhead" and "Lost Highway" were less successful, but no less controversial. Lynch is everything an Aquarian visionary should be. His risk-taking career has been built on the hope that his intensely personal vision will somehow connect with the paying public. Nobody else makes movies like his. Nobody would. Or could.

**Suggested Rental:** "The Elephant Man" (1980)
Nominated for eight Oscars (including Best Picture and Best Director), this is the movie that made Lynch mainstream (well, relatively speaking). It's an astonishing picture, an eminently Victorian fable about the triumph of the human spirit over this too, too solid flesh, as embodied in the twisted form of John Merrick, an actual nineteenth-century freak. Lynch renders Merrick's story in scrupulously Victorian tones. Saved from a degrading life as a sideshow freak by a London surgeon (Anthony Hopkins), Merrick (John Hurt) became the toast of the town – a celebrated figure as revered by royalty as he was once reviled by the London low-life. Lynch uses Merrick's passion play as a means to examine the psyche of an era – the lace doilies on Jack the Ripper's armchair. In doing so, he reveals his Aquarian humanitarianism, which is as essential to his art as his Aquarian strangeness.

**Aquarian Moment:** Just about everything David Lynch says is an Aquarian moment. Consider this vision of the Industrial Revolution vis-à-vis Merrick's deformity: "Big explosions always reminded me of those papillomatous growths . . . they were like slow explosions. And they started erupting from the bone. . . . So the idea of smokestacks and soot and industry next to this flesh got me going. Human beings are like little factories." Aquarians will understand this better than most of us.

## Paul Newman (January 26, 1925)

He is the true rebel without a cause. On-screen, that is. Whether playing Hud or Fast Eddie, Butch Cassidy or Cool Hand Luke, there's something in Paul Newman's characters that impels them to go against authority. It's the same impulse that defines the alcoholic lawyer in "The Verdict," the charmer-at-twilight in "Nobody's Fool" and the consummate con artist in "The Sting." Yet that's only half of Newman's thoroughly Aquarian personality. Off-screen, he's the rebel *with* a cause — a dozen causes. An outspoken liberal, he's lent his voice (and considerable financial backing) to a variety of charities and political do-gooders. And he's managed to do so without attracting the ire and/or scorn that hounds the similarly motivated Vanessa Redgrave. Essentially, Newman has done it right, transforming his early boyish charm into aged-to-perfection longevity. One of a kind — and one with a heart.

**Suggested Rental:** "Butch Cassidy and the Sundance Kid" (1968)

Even though it has horses and cowboy boots and six-shooters, this movie was always less about the West than it was about the late '60s (and Aquarians know what that means). Newman and Robert Redford are a perfect match as the title characters — two amiable outlaws who see themselves as latter-day Robin Hoods; that is, they take from the rich (the railroads) and give to the poor (themselves). Katharine Ross comes along for the ride but as Newman himself pointed out, she's pretty disposable. The core of the film is the relationship between the two guys who come off as pure Aquarians in nature — doggedly individualistic, mildly eccentric and generally good-natured. True, the movie coasts by on its stars' considerable charm. But let's face it: Newman and Redford are most pleasant company as they toss around William Goldman's anachronistic banter with matinee-idol aplomb.

**Aquarian Moment:** Though their characters were famously freeze-framed at the end of the movie, getting shot up in Bolivia, both Newman and Redford have kept Butch and Sundance "alive" as the trademarks of each man's major charitable institution. Redford created the Sundance Institute, which has long championed the cause of independent films. Newman's camp for kids with leukemia is called the Hole in the Wall Camp. Movie myth-making meets Aquarian humanitarianism. Nice mix.

## François Truffaut (Febraury 6, 1932)

Even those who don't necessarily know Truffaut's work as a director will recognize him as the passionately humanistic, ever-questing scientist in Steven Spielberg's "Close Encounters of the Third Kind." Well, kids, it was typecasting. As movie critic (for the Cahiers du Cinema in the '50s), movie director (more than thirty films before his death at age fifty-two) and movie lover extraordinaire, Truffaut was infallibly open-minded and compassionate. He never lost that childlike sense of wonder about the world and about the movies. In true Aquarian fashion, his films reach out to an audience with open arms and an open heart. Whether contemplating the mystery of childhood ("Small Change," "The Wild Child"), the mystery of women ("The Man Who Loved Women," "Jules and Jim"), or the mystery of make-believe ("Day for Night," "The Last Metro"), he's the man who loved movies.

**Suggested Rental:** "The Last Metro" (1980)
Set in a Paris theater during the German Occupation, this superb movie's theme is the nature of commitment — to matters of conscience (hello, Aquarius) as well as to matters of greasepaint. Actress/manager Catherine Deneuve keeps the curtain up while her Jewish husband, a famous director, hides

under his own stage. Gerard Depardieu is the company's new leading man who moonlights with the Resistance. What Truffaut is exploring (with his customary Aquarian humanity) is the delicate nature of collaboration – how and when people take stands. The movie is theatrical about its acts of courage and courageous about its unabashed theatricality. We see that in the best of times and in the worst of times, some people simply behave better than others. We also learn there can be threads of defiance in the most seemingly aquiescent acts – something Aquarians already knew.

**Aquarian Moment:** The movie was one of the director's biggest commercial successes, but some critics took him to task for not being "hard" enough on the harsh realities of the Occupation. Truffaut was only eight years old when the Nazis invaded his homeland and his defense had the gentle insight of an Aquarian truth-seeker: "I filled out the screenplay with details that had struck me in my childhood . . . there you have what 'The Last Metro' probably is: the theater and the Occupation seen by a child."

## MOVIES "BORN" AS AQUARIANS

BILL AND TED'S EXCELLENT
  ADVENTURE
STANLEY AND IRIS
L.A. STORY
SLEEPING WITH THE ENEMY
THE SILENCE OF THE LAMBS
WAYNE'S WORLD
MATINEE
SOMERSBY
GROUNDHOG DAY
ACE VENTURA, PET
  DETECTIVE

REALITY BITES
MURDER IN THE FIRST
BEFORE SUNRISE
BOYS ON THE SIDE
THE QUICK AND THE DEAD
THE BRADY BUNCH MOVIE
BEAUTIFUL GIRLS
FIERCE CREATURES
ABSOLUTE POWER
SPICE WORLD

# OTHER FAMOUS AQUARIANS

**JANUARY 20**
Skeet Ulrich (1969)
David Lynch (1946)
Patricia Neal (1926)
DeForest Kelley (1920)
Federico Fellini (1920)
Colin Clive (1898)
George Burns (1896)
Finlay Currie (1876)

*Geena Davis*

**JANUARY 21**
Geena Davis (1957)
Robby Benson (1956)
Jill Eikenberry (1946)
Ann Wedgeworth (1935)
Steve Reeves (1926)
Telly Savalas (1924)
Paul Scofield (1922)
J. Carrol Nash (1900)

**JANUARY 22**
Balthazar Getty (1975)
Olivia D'Abo (1967)
Linda Blair (1959)
Ann Southern (1909)
Conrad Veight (1893)
D.W. Griffith (1875)

**JANUARY 23**
Rutger Hauer (1944)
Jeanne Moreau (1928)
Ernie Kovacs (1919)
Dan Duryea (1907)
Humphrey Bogart (1899)
Sergei Eisenstein (1898)
Randolph Scott (1898)
Franklin Pangborn (1893)

**JANUARY 24**
Nastassia Kinski (1960)
Michael Ontkean (1950)
Daniel Auteuil (1950)
John Belushi (1949)
Sharon Tate (1943)
Ernest Borgnine (1917)
Ann Todd (1909)
Estelle Winwood (1883)

**JANUARY 25**
Leigh Taylor-Young (1944)
Dean Jones (1931)
Mildred Dunnock (1904)
Diana Hyland (1936)

**JANUARY 26**
Ellen Degeneres (1958)
Patrick Dewaere (1947)
Scott Glenn (1941)
Henry Jaglom (1941)
Roger Vadim (1928)
Paul Newman (1925)
William Hopper (1915)

*James Cromwell*

## JANUARY 27
Tamlyn Tomita (1966)
Bridget Fonda (1964)
Mimi Rogers (1956)
Mikhail Baryshnikov (1948)
James Cromwell (1942)
Troy Donahue (1936)
Donna Reed (1921)
Sabu (1924)

*Alan Alda*

## JANUARY 28
Elijah Wood (1981)
Harley Jane Kozak (1957)
Marthe Keller (1945)
Alan Alda (1936)
Ernst Lubitsch (1892)

## JANUARY 29
Oprah Winfrey (1954)
Marc Singer (1948)
Tom Sellek (1945)
Katharine Ross (1942)

Paddy Chayesky (1923)
John Forsythe (1918)
Victor Mature (1915)
W.C. Fields (1879)

## JANUARY 30
Christian Bale (1974)
Charles Dutton (1951)
Nick Broomfield (1948)
Vanessa Redgrave (1937)
Gene Hackman (1930)
John Ireland (1914)
David Wayne (1914)

## JANUARY 31
Anthony LaPlagia (1959)
Derek Jarman (1942)
Suzanne Pleshette (1937)
James Franciscus (1934)
Jean Simmons (1929)
Joanne Dru (1923)
Mario Lanza (1921)
John Agar (1921)
Tallulah Bankhead (1903)
Eddie Cantor (1892)

## FEBRUARY 1
Pauly Shore (1968)
Brandon Lee (1965)
Sherilyn Fenn (1965)
Terry Jones (1942)
Stuart Whitman (1926)
George Pal (1908)
Clark Gable (1901)
John Ford (1895)

# AQUARIUS

## FEBRUARY 2
Brent Spiner (1949)
Farrah Fawcett (1947)
Bo Hopkins (1942)
Tom Smothers (1937)
Bonita Granville (1923)

## FEBRUARY 3
Keith Gordon (1961)
Nathan Lane (1956)
Lizzie Borden (1950)
Blythe Danner (1943)
Victor Buono (1938)
Peggy Ann Garner (1932)
Kenneth Anger (1930)

## FEBRUARY 4
Gabrielle Anwar (1971)
Lisa Eichhorn (1952)
George Romero (1940)
Ida Lupino (1918)

## FEBRUARY 5
Jennifer Jason Leigh (1962)
Christopher Guest (1948)
Barbara Hershey (1948)
Charlotte Rampling (1948)
Michael Mann (1943)
Red Buttons (1919)
John Carradine (1906)

## FEBRUARY 6
Jason Gedrick (1965)
James Spader (1960)
Barry Miller (1958)
Francois Truffaut (1932)

Rip Torn (1931)
Mamie Van Doren (1931)
Zsa Zsa Gabor (1917)
Ronald Reagan (1911)
Ramon Novarro (1899)
Elmo Lincoln (1899)

## FEBRUARY 7
Tina Majorino (1985)
Hector Babenco (1946)
Buster Crabbe (1908)
Jock Mahoney (1919)

## FEBRUARY 8
Mary McCormack (1969)
Mary Steenburgen (1953)
Brooke Adams (1949)
Nick Nolte (1940)
James Dean (1931)
Stanley Baker (1927)
Jack Lemmon (1925)
Lana Turner (1920)
Betty Field (1913)
King Vidor (1894)
Edith Evans (1888)

## FEBRUARY 9
Jaco Van Dormael (1957)
Mia Farrow (1945)
Joe Pesci (1943)
Janet Suzman (1939)
Carmen Miranda (1909)
Brian Donlevy (1901)
Ronald Colman (1891)

## FEBRUARY 10
Laura Dern (1967)
Michael Apted (1941)
Robert Wagner (1930)
Lon Chaney Jr. (1906)
John Farrow (1904)
Judith Anderson (1898)
Jimmy Durante (1893)

*Jennifer Aniston*

## FEBRUARY 11
Jennifer Aniston (1969)
Burt Reynolds (1936)
Leslie Nielsen (1926)
Kim Stanley (1925)
Eva Gabor (1920)
Joseph L. Mankiewicz (1909)

## FEBRUARY 12
Christina Ricci (1980)
Cliff De Young (1945)
Maud Adams (1945)
Joe Don Baker (1936)
Franco Zeffirelli (1923)

## FEBRUARY 13
Bibi Anderson (1954)
Stockard Channing (1944)
Carol Lynley (1942)
Oliver Reed (1936)

George Segal (1934)
Kim Novak (1933)

## FEBRUARY 14
Meg Tilly (1960)
Gregory Hines (1946)
Alan Parker (1944)
Vic Morrow (1932)
Thelma Ritter (1905)
Nigel Bruce 91895)
Jack Benny (1844)

## FEBRUARY 15
Chris Farley (1964)
Jane Seymour (1951)
Richard Marquand (1938)
Claire Bloom (1931)
Kevin McCarthy (1914)
Cesar Romero (1907)
Gale Sondergaard (1899)
John Barrymore (1882)

## FEBRUARY 16
Ice-T (1958)
Brian Bedford (1935)
Vera-Ellen (1926)
Sonny Bono (1935)
LeVar Burton (1957)

## FEBRUARY 17
Lou Diamond Phillips (1962)
Rene Russo (1954)
Brenda Fricker (1945)
Alan Bates (1934)
Hal Holbrook (1925)
Arthur Kennedy (1914)

**FEBRAURY 18**
Molly Ringwald (1968)
Matt Dillon (1964)
Greta Scacchi (1960)
John Travolta (1954)
John Hughes (1950)
Cybill Shepherd (1950)
Sinead Cusack (1948)
Istvan Szabo (1938)
Mary Ure (1933)
George Kennedy (1925)
Jack Palance (1919)
Adolphe Menjou (1890)

# PISCES

## FEBRUARY 19 — MARCH 20

Pisceans are the dreamers of the zodiac. Not sleepy-heads — just drifty and extremely intuitive. Their innate empathy translates into a gift for interpretation that makes them a natural for the movies. Bluntly put, Pisces people are so sensitive that they're not only totally in touch with their own feelings, but, chances are, they're more in touch with your feelings than you are.

That's what's makes them such superlative actors — that and their untrammeled imagination. Chameleon-like, they can assume a persona that has nothing to do with the soft-focus label that's usually assigned to their sign. Think Sharon Stone, Glenn Close or Bruce Willis. Think Jackie Gleason, Michael Caine or Kurt Russell.

What Pisces performers have is an innate ability to transform into whatever people want (or need) them to be. Thus, the utter melding of actor and image: Rex Harrison's crisp urbanity or Lee Marvin's roughneck tough guy; saintly Sidney Poitier or sultry Jean Harlow.

That interpretive thing works on a larger scale, too. A surprising number of movie directors are born under Pisces. Consider this list: Spike Lee, Jonathan Demme, John Frankenheimer, Neil Jordan, Bernardo Bertolucci, Mike Leigh, Wolfgang Peterson, Renny Harlin, Luis Bunuel, Martin Ritt, Adrian Lynne, George Miller, Ron Howard and Rob Reiner. Add in such notorious "softies" as David Cronenberg and Sam Peckinpah (right . . . ). And let's not forget the greatest auteur alive — if you ask the French — Jerry Lewis.

As a movie-goer, Pisces isn't much into reality, so forget the documentary section. Violence isn't their thing either, even if Chuck Norris is a Pisces. But remember Pisces' symbol: the two fishes. Water is their element, so you probably couldn't go wrong with "Jaws," "Endless Summer," "The Little Mermaid" or "A Fish Called Wanda." Spiritually themed films have an appeal as well. Traditionalists may want to check out "Made in Heaven" or "Heaven Can Wait." Nontraditionalists might try "Kundun," or "Seven Years in Tibet."

Remember, Pisces wants to feel your pain. And your love. That's probably why Piscean Elizabeth Taylor got married so many times.

## FIVE SUGGESTED RENTALS

**"The Purple Rose of Cairo"** (1985)
Woody Allen's brilliant, bittersweet fable about reality versus illusion and the seductive promises in the dark the movies make. Mia Farrow has the Pisces part — a dreamy depression waif who escapes the hard facts of her life with brutish husband Danny Aiello by drinking in the glamorous fictions offered by Hollywood. Her particular passion is an archly art-deco comedy called "The Purple Rose of Cairo," starring pith-helmeted adventurer, Tom Baxter (Jeff Daniels). One day,

Tom simply steps off the screen and into her life (a pure Pisces moment). Havoc ensues, both for the other characters stranded midscreen and for the real-life actor (also Daniels) who plays Tom and fears this could ruin his career. It's a Piscean salute to the poetic and impractical, as well as a needed reminder that things don't always work out in life the way they do in movies.

### "Night of the Shooting Stars" (1982)
If you haven't heard of the Taviani brothers, now's the time, especially if you're a Pisces. Their film is a fairy-tale epic about some Italian villagers who set off in the waning days of World War II to hook up with the promised American liberators. The movie is told as a bedtime story to a little girl, and events are filtered through the memory of the storyteller, herself a girl of six at the time (thus making the whole movie an act of interpretation). The radiant result is oral tradition transfixed on film – embellished reality with an overlay of child-like wonder (sound familiar, Pisces?). The title refers to the Night of San Lorenzo when, according to Italian tradition, wishes come true. Fanciful, brutal, sentimental, earthy and lyrical all at once, this rare, exquisite film is like watching poetry in motion. In motion pictures, that is.

### "Heavenly Creatures" (1994)
Based on the true story of New Zealand's most sensational murder case, this is a tale of make-believe gone mad, of fantasy turned fatal (have I got your attention, Pisces?). In the '50s, two schoolgirls – chubby, sullen Pauline (Melanie Lynskey) and brash, worldly Juliet (Kate Winslet) – discover a mutual passion for Mario Lanza and a mutual disdain for the rest of the world. Soon, they've concocted a complicated fantasy world with giant butterflies, princesses, knights and Orson Welles. It's a riveting portrait of overheated adolescence run amok. Together, the two create a kind of codependent hysteria; if they were living in sixteenth-century

Salem, they'd be fingering witches. Part "The World of Henry Orient," part Leopold and Loeb, this film is as swooningly self-intoxicating as its schoolgirl protagonists.

**"Melvin and Howard"** (1980)
Remember Melvin Dummar, the guy who claimed to have discovered the so-called "Mormon will" left by Howard Hughes? Maybe he wasn't a Pisces in real life, but he certainly comes off as a prime example in Jonathan Demme's splendid human comedy. Demme takes the supposed desert meeting between Melvin (Paul Le Mat), a sometime gas-station attendant and full-time goofball, and the amazing Mr. Hughes (an amazing Jason Robards) as a jumping-off place for a delightfully daffy trip through the fads and foibles of the American Dream, from sea to shining Sea World. In essence, it's a loving look at what makes true believers, whether it's a lovable loser and improbable optimist like Melvin, or his on-again, off-again wife (Mary Steenburgen in an Oscar-winning performance), who's as comfortable dancing in a strip joint as she is being a game-show contestant.

**"Therese"** (1986)
This one's for that inescapably mystic side of Pisces. Therese Martin died in a French convent in 1897 and was made a saint in 1925. In Alain Cavalier's visionary and subversive film, Therese (Catherine Mouchet) comes off as a kind of Moonie-nun for whom the mortifications of the flesh are a balm to the spirit (hairshirt, anyone?) Her nunnery is like a fervid fan club for Jesus; the sisters are as ga-ga for Christ as groupies swooning over Leonardo DiCaprio. Yet Cavalier doesn't just make fun of them. His tone is a mixture of bemusement and benediction as he shows us the radiant mystery of faith — something that's often a little less mysterious to Pisceans than to the rest of us. He wants us to see what's funny, frightening and, finally, fulfilling about a life lived in the purity of belief. Ultimately, he says, only Heaven

knows what makes a saint tick. All we can do is have faith in her faith.

## SIX TALENTED PISCEANS

### Elizabeth Taylor (February 27, 1932)

She was once the most beautiful girl in the world, and she has the husbands and the jewels to prove it. But Taylor's relentless campaign on behalf of AIDS research proves her beauty is far more than skin deep. Her focus, her vitality, her love of the spotlight, her sheer survivalist skills — none of these traits would suggest your typical Pisces. But it's that Pisces ability to somehow float through life that has kept her in the public eye for so long. That, along with her Pisces compassion, intuitiveness and creativity. Whether she was playing dream girls ("A Place in the Sun"), shrews ("Who's Afraid of Virginia Woolf?" ) or sex goddesses ("Cleopatra"), she was always a commanding presence . And that natural Pisces aversion to reality was something Taylor handled effortlessly. She simply made her real life ten times more interesting than any movie.

**Suggested Rental:** "National Velvet" (1944)

It's still Taylor's favorite movie even though she was only twelve years old when she made it. She plays Velvet Brown, a horse-crazy English girl who dreams of riding her steed — an unruly beast called The Pie (In Enid Bagnold's book, he's a piebald, but in the movie he's played by a chestnut named Sir Charles, making the name rather odd) — in the Grand National, a famous and often deadly steeplechase. One problem: girls weren't allowed to be jockeys then. But with the help of her trainer (Mickey Rooney), she disguises herself as a boy and enters the race. Her attachment to her dream has a mystical force that's pure Pisces; she's almost beside herself with her need to see this thing through. Elizabeth/Velvet comes off as emotional, impractical, impulsive, unrealistic and often childish. She also comes off a winner – in the film and in her career.

**Piscean Moment:** Pisces are often thought to have special, almost mystical powers. It's said that when Taylor, who was convinced that she was born to play Velvet, first approached producer Pandro S. Berman, he thought she was too small, too slight and too delicate. She vowed she'd grow and she did – reportedly stretching three inches in just twelve weeks. Now that's Piscean mind over matter.

## Billy Crystal (March 14, 1947)

The funny thing about Billy Crystal isn't just how funny he is. It's how he manages to come off as sweetly romantic without seeming all icky-gooey. A lot of that comes from his Piscean sensitivity. Crystal can do schtick with the best of them – TV's first gay character on "Soap;" dozens of memorable bits during his stint on "Saturday Night Live;" a devil in a smoking jacket in "Deconstructing Harry." But the roles we remember best are the urban cowboy undergoing a midlife crisis in "City Slickers," the aging bitter comic in "Mr. Saturday Night" and the mixed-up charmer in "When Harry Met Sally . . ." What sets Crystal apart is that Piscean need to connect. He is, like most Pisces, a giver. Think of his on-going commitment to Comic Relief. And his willingness to endure that annual trial-by-fire known as hosting the Oscars, well, it verges on the saintly.

**Suggested Rental:** "Forget Paris" (1995)
Forget that it wasn't a big hit in theaters. Crystal is in peak form in this bright, engaging romantic comedy that dares to ask the question: can love survive marriage? Crystal and

Debra Winger meet in Paris, spend an idyllic week together and eventually get married. And that's where the story that begins as happily-ever-after takes a clubbing from such '90s pressures as a two-career marriage, infertility problems, etc. Rendered in a manner reminscent of "Broadway Danny Rose" and "The Princess Bride" — that is, as a tale told — the movie's able cast of story-tellers includes Joe Mantegna, Richard Masur and Julie Kavner. Think of it as a kind of sequel to "When Harry Met Sally . . ." More like, "When Harry Wed Sally." And that's a whole new ball game — a hard dose of reality that Piscean romantics will find awfully familiar because, for them, reality can be so unfamiliar . . .

**Piscean Moment:** Crystal got the idea for the movie from his own long-standing marriage (over a quarter of a century). He told an interviewer that he wanted to explore what happens "when the honeymoon's over and the marriage begins. . . . How much of yourself do you give up for the sake of a relationship? How many times can you reinvent yourself to try to please somebody else?" A purely Pisces bit of self-expression: insecure yet totally in touch with his feelings . . . and his wife's feelings.

### Sharon Stone (March 10, 1958)

Like her sex-goddess colleague, Elizabeth Taylor, Sharon Stone doesn't initially seem the Pisces type. She's too aggressive, too focused, too icy (after all, it was that ice pick in "Basic Instinct" that helped make her a star). But like Taylor, she's never allowed her astonishing beauty to overwhelm her Piscean intuition. An "overnight sensation" who took twelve years to happen, Stone is a stay-er. Again, that doesn't sound like our easily distracted, passive Pisces. But remember, Pisces are natural born actors, and Stone's need to work in movies is almost palpable. If you're only familiar with her "Basic Instinct/Sliver" persona, check her out as a hilariously conniving starlet in "Irreconcilable Differences" or as a daring photojournalist in "Year of the Gun." And don't forget her savvy, Oscar-nominated turn as mobster Robert De Niro's drug-addict wife in "Casino."

**Suggested Rental:** "The Quick and the Dead" (1995)
A dead-on, over-the-top Western from Sam "Evil Dead" Raimi. Gene Hackman reprises his avuncular villainy from "Unforgiven" as the Big Cheese in a small western town who, for his own amusement and ego-gratification, sponsors an annual quick-draw competition. Among the gathering of gunfighters lured by money, glory or both are a flashy gambler (Lance Henriksen), a pipe-smoking hired gun (David Keith) and a cocky kid (Leonardo DiCaprio) who happens to be Hackman's son. There's also a mysterious stranger (Stone) with an old score to settle, and a pre-"L.A. Confidential" Russell Crowe as a former gun-slinger who's found religion, but is still forced by Hackman to compete (draw or die). The movie is like an overheated homage to Sergio Leone's spaghetti westerns. And Stone, who produced, is obviously fulfilling a fantasy – she gets the Clint Eastwood role, right down to the cheroot and the sneer.

**Piscean Moment:** To continue the Liz Taylor synchronicity . . . young Elizabeth fell in love with her steed in "National Velvet," and at the end of the shoot, after some not-so-subtle lobbying, she was able to get producer Berman to give him to her. Stone also fell for her equine costar – a looker named Magic – but being the film's producer as well as its star, she didn't have to beg anyone in order to take him home.

# Drew Barrymore (February 22, 1975)

When Pisces are good, they're very, very good. Near saints, in fact. But when they're bad . . . they can be devious and prone to every addiction under the sun. Drew

Barrymore, scion of the world's most famous acting dynasty, made her movie debut at age two and a half, had her first glass of champagne at age eight, had tried cocaine by age eleven and was in re-hab by age thirteen. No wonder she called her memoir — written when she was a ripe old fifteen — "Little Girl Lost." But the erstwhile tabloid princess has made a remarkable recovery, a tribute to her Piscean need to be creative above all else. She's done impressive work in some respectable films ("Bad Girls," "Boys on the Side," "The Wedding Singer") and has added another bonafide block-buster ("Scream") to her resume. She's had her share of Piscean lows; let's see how she handles some Piscean highs — the legal ones, that is.

**Suggested Rental:** "E.T. — The Extraterrestrial" (1982)
Clap your hands if you believe in fairies, friendly aliens and, most especially Steven Spielberg. The movie, which remains Spielberg's favorite, is an enchanting inversion of Peter Pan, in which Earth serves as a kind of Neverland for a small vis-itor from another planet who finds a safe refuge with a lost boy named Elliott (Henry Thomas). Note how well Spielberg understands our slumbering child selves — something he shares with Pisces — how smoothly he interweaves references to children's classics of every sort with the familiar cultural clutter of early '80s suburbia. Elliott and E.T. behave like psychic Piscean twins, totally in touch with each other and with anyone else who could use a little out-of-this-world uplift. As Elliott's little sister, Gertie, Barrymore gives off the most memorable movie squeal this side of Julia Roberts in "Pretty Woman."

**Piscean Moment:** Casting Barrymore was easy; according to Spielberg, she stood out from the hundreds of other tots by reciting made-up stories about being in a punk band. But coming up with E.T's look was more difficult. He finally found it by pasting a cut-out of Carl Sandburg's eyes over the face of a small child. Talk about Pisces incarnate – an old soul with a young spirit.

## Holly Hunter (March 20, 1958)

She's a New South spitfire who became the first actress since Jane Wyman in "Johnny Belinda" to win an Oscar without saying a word. As the mute music-lover in "The Piano," she won over audiences and Oscar-voters with her fierce body language and sheer intensity. How can this possibly be the same actress who first made her mark as the driven, nervy television producer in "Broadcast News?" Or played Tom Cruise's whacky, gum-snapping secretary in "The Firm?" Or the kid-obsessed cop in "Raising Arizona?" Or the feisty romantic lead in "Always?" Hunter defies typecasting not only through her talent, but through her Piscean ability to channel her emotional intuitiveness into an astonishing range of roles. Here's one fish who refuses to be hooked by Hollywood narrow-mindedness.

**Suggested Rental:** "The Piano" (1993)

The movie that won Hunter her long-deserved Oscar is hauntingly erotic, full-throttle romantic and exquisitely mysterious. Director Jane Campion brings her dazzlingly original vision and genuinely eccentric sensibility to a romance as gloriously gothic in its own strange way as "Wuthering Heights." Think David Lean meets David Lynch. Hunter plays Ada, a mute Scottish widow who, in the 1850s, travels with her small daughter (another Oscar-winner, Anna Paquin) to New Zealand and an arranged marriage with a rich landowner (Sam Neill). The twist comes when her husband sells her beloved piano to his gone-native neighbor (a tattooed Harvey Keitel) who uses the instrument as bartering material in a bold, sensual and increasingly dangerous courtship. "The Piano" may strike simple chords, but it resonates with complex themes and emotions. Its innate oddness makes it a very Piscean love story.

**Piscean Moment:** Much like Elizabeth Taylor and "National Velvet," Hunter felt she was born to play Ada. Something of a stretch since Campion envisioned her as tall (Hunter is 5' 2") and extraordinarily beautiful (Hunter is more cute as a button). But she persisted and, while she didn't have to grow three inches, she grew in Campion's mind, slowly replacing the fimmaker's original conception. That's a Pisces at work — that ability to so translate herself into someone else that she and the role became as one. Campion never stood a chance.

## Ron Howard (March 1, 1954)

How in the world did little Opie on "The Andy Griffith Show" grow up to be one of the most successful and respected directors in Hollywood? More to the point, how did Ron Howard make it look so easy? One day he was wandering around in faux '50s duds for "Happy Days;" the next he had accumulated a solid directing resume ("Cocoon," "Parenthood," "Ransom"), a Director's Guild of America award ("Apollo 13") and a slew of Oscar nominations ("Apollo 13"). Sure, auteurists sneer that his work doesn't have any distinctive personality, but that's part of his Pisces nature — changeable, empathetic, impressionable. A story about Irish immigrants ("Far and Away") brings out one side, while one about firefighters ("Backdraft") brings out another. He's a prime example of a Pisces swimming confidently in the mainstream.

**Suggested Rental:** "Splash" (1982)
A fantasy fish-story . . . how much more Piscean can a movie get? Howard created a first-rate comedy/fantasy/romance about a mermaid (Daryl Hannah) who falls for a mortal (Tom Hanks) and follows him to Manhattan. On dry land, she sprouts legs, so

Hanks doesn't realize he's in love with a Mrs. Paul's doll. However, scientist Eugene Levy smells something fishy and spends most of the movie trying to expose this Chick of the Sea (he's like a frizzy-haired Wile E. Coyote). Hanks, in his first important role, already shows that everyman lovableness that would make him huge star, while Hannah is perfect as the dish out of water - a fine physical comedian with Lady Godiva locks and an incandescent smile. Still, they almost get the movie stolen out from under them by that rock-candy mountain of comic humanity, John Candy, who play's Hanks' ne'er-do-well brother.

**Piscean Moment:** Hanks recalls that he showed up on the set one day without knowing either the production schedule or his lines. So the scene took a lot longer to shoot than necessary. But when it was over, instead of screaming at him, Howard merely said, "You know you should've been a little more prepared." It's that Piscean intuitiveness; the director knew that yelling at an insecure young actor would simply freeze him up. Instead, he let him know that a starring role means certain responsibilities. It was a lesson, Hanks says, that he never forgot.

## MOVIES "BORN" UNDER PISCES

THE HUNT FOR RED
  OCTOBER
HE SAID, SHE SAID
THE DOORS
MY COUSIN VINNIE
BASIC INSTINCT
FALLING DOWN
SWING KIDS
RICH IN LOVE
DANGEROUS BEAUTY
THE REF

NAKED GUN 33⅓
THE SECRET OF ROAN
  INNISH
OUTBREAK
PRIMARY COLORS
BEFORE AND AFTER
UP CLOSE AND PERSONAL
DARK CITY
THE BIRDCAGE
DONNIE BRASCO
PRIVATE PARTS

# OTHER FAMOUS PISCES

*Jeff Daniels*

**FEBRUARY 19**
Kathleen Beller (1956)
Jeff Daniels (1955)
John Frankenheimer (1930)
Lee Marvin (1924)
Merle Oberon (1911)
Louis Calhern (1895)
Cedric Hardwicke (1893)

**FEBRUARY 20**
Lili Taylor (1967)
Imogen Stubbs (1961)
Mike Leigh (1943)
Robert Altman (1925)
Sidney Poitier (1924)
Jean Negulesco (1900)

**FEBRUARY 21**
William Baldwin (1963)
Christopher Atkins (1961)
Alan Rickman (1946)
David Geffin (1943)
John McEnery (1940)
Sam Peckinpah (1925)
Ann Sheridan (1915)
Zachary Scott (1914)

**FEBRUARY 22**
Drew Barrymore (1975)
Julie Waters (1950)
Miou-Miou (1950)
Jonathan Demme (1944)
Paul Dooley (1928)
John Mills (1908)
Luis Bunuel (1900)
Dwight Frye (1899)

**FEBRUARY 23**
Peter Fonda (1940)
Norman Taurog (1899)
Jiri Menzel (1938)
Diane Varsi (1938)

**FEBRUARY 24**
Billy Zane (1970)
Helen Shaver (1951)
Abe Vigoda (19210
Marjorie Main (1890)
Michael Radford (1946)

**FEBRAURY 25**
Sean Astin (1971)
Neil Jordan (1950)
Tom Courtenay (1937)
Jim Backus (1913)
Gert Frobe (1913)
Zeppo Marx (1901)

**FEBRUARY 26**
Bill Duke (1943)
Godfrey Cambridge (1933)

Betty Hutton (1921)
Tony Randall (1920)
Margaret Leighton (1922)
Jackie Gleason (1916)
Tex Avery (1908)

*Joanne Woodward*

## FEBRUARY 27
Adam Baldwin (1962)
Elizabeth Taylor (1932)
Joanne Woodward (1930)
Joan Bennett (1910)
Franchot Tone (1905)
William Demarest (1892)

## FEBRUARY 28
Robert Sean Leonard (1969)
Rae Dawn Chong (1962)
John Turturro (1957)
Dorothy Stratton (1960)
Bernadette Peters (1948)
Mercedes Ruehl (1948)
Tommy Tune (1939)
Charles Durning (1923)
Zero Mostel (1915)
Vincente Minnelli (1910)

## FEBRUARY 29
Denis Farina (1944)
Alex Rocca (1936)

Joss Ackland (1928)
William Wellman (1896)

## MARCH 1
Ron Howard (1954)
Roger Daltrey (1944)
Raymond St. Jacques (1930)
Jacques Rivette (1928)
Harry Belafonte (1927)
Jack Clayton (1921)
David Niven (1910)
Lionel Atwill (1885)

## MARCH 2
Jon Bon Jovi (1962)
Laraine Newman (1952)
Jennifer Jones (1919)
Desi Arnaz (1917)
Martin Ritt (1914)

## MARCH 3
Miranda Richardson (1958)
George Miller (1945)
Jean Harlow (1911)
Canada Lee (1907)

## MARCH 4
Patsy Kensit (1968)
Kelly Lynch (1959)
Catherine O'Hara (1954)
Halle Gerima (1946)
Adrian Lynne (1941)
Paula Prentiss (1939)
John Garfield (1913)
Pearl White (1889)

## MARCH 5
Penn Jillette (1955)
Samantha Eggar (1939)
Dean Stockwell (1936)
Jack Cassidy (1927)
Rex Harrison (1908)

## MARCH 6
Shaquille O'Neal (1972)
Moira Kelly (1968)
Rob Reiner (1945)
Lou Costello (1906)

## MARCH 7
John Heard (1946)
Daniel J. Travanti (1940)
James Broderick (1927)
Anna Magnani (1908)

## MARCH 8
Kathy Ireland (1963)
Aidan Quinn (1959)
Mickey Dolenz (1945)
Lynn Redgrave (1943)
Cyd Charisse (1921)
Alan Hale, Jr. (1918)
Claire Trevor (1909)
Sam Jaffe (1891)

## MARCH 9
Juliette Binoche (1965)
Linda Fiorentino (1960)
Ornella Muti (1955)
Trish Van Devere (1945)
Raul Julia (1940)
Irene Pappas (1926)

Will Geer (1902)

## MARCH 10
Jasmine Guy (1964)
Sharon Stone (1958)
Katharine Houghton (1945)
Chuck Norris (1940)
Gregory La Cava (1892)
Barry Fitzgerald (1888)

## MARCH 11
Thora Birch (1982)
Jerry Zucker (1950)
Dominique Sanda (1946)
Tom Savini (1946)
Albert Salmi (1928)
Dorothy Gish (1898)
Raoul Walsh (1892)

## MARCH 12
Courtney B. Vance (1960)
Liza Minnelli (1946)
Gordon MacRae (1921)
James Taylor (1948)

## MARCH 13
Annabeth Gish (1971)
Dana Delany (1956)
Glenne Headly (1955)
William H. Macy (1950)
Andre Techine (1943)
Henry Hathaway (1898)

## MARCH 14
Billy Crystal (1947)
Rita Tushingham (1942)

Wolfgang Peterson (1941)
Raymond J. Barry (1939)
Bertrand Blier (1939)
Michael Caine (1933)
Quincy Jones (1933)

## MARCH 15
Renny Harlin (1959)
Craig Wasson (1954)
David Cronenberg (1943)
Judd Hirsch (1935)
Macdonald Carey (1913)
George Brent (1904)

## MARCH 16
Isabelle Huppert (1955)
Kate Nelligan (1951)
Victor Garber (1949)
Erik Estrada (1949)
Bernardo Bertolucci (1940)
Jerry Lewis (1926)
Leo McKern (1920)

*Kurt Russell*

## MARCH 17
Rob Lowe (1964)
Casey Siemaszko (1961)
Gary Sinise (1955)
Leslie-Anne Down (1954)
Kurt Russell (1951)

Rudolf Nureyev (1938)
Mercedes McCambridge (1918)
Shemp Howard (1895)

## MARCH 18
Queen Latifah (1970)
Irene Cara (1963)
Vanessa L. Williams (1963)
Luc Besson (1959)
Brad Dourif (1950)
Smiley Burnette (1911)
Robert Donat (1905)
Edward Everett Horton (1886)

*Glenn Close*

## MARCH 19
Bruce Willis (1955)
Glenn Close (1947)
Ursula Andress (1936)
Renee Taylor (1935)
Patrick McGoohan (1928)
Louis Hayward (1909)

## MARCH 20
Holly Hunter (1958)
Theresa Russell (1957)
Spike Lee (1957)
William Hurt (1950)
Carl Reiner (1922)

# PISCES

Wendell Corey (1914)
Michael Redgrave (1908)
Edgar Buchanan (1903)